DATE DUE			

Small Countries,
Large Issues

Small Countries, Large Issues

Studies in U.S.-Latin American Asymmetries

Mark Falcoff

American Enterprise Institute for Public Research
Washington and London

Mark Falcoff, a resident fellow at AEI's Center for Hemispheric Studies, has taught at the Universities of Illinois, Oregon, and California
(Los Angeles) and at the U.S. Foreign Service Institute; he served as a
senior consultant to the National Bipartisan Commission on Central
America.

Library of Congress Cataloging in Publication Data

Falcoff, Mark.
  Small countries, large issues.

  (AEI studies ; 409)
  1. Latin America—Foreign relations—United States.
  2. United States—Foreign relations—Latin America.
  3. Latin America—Politics and government—1948-.
  I. Title. II. Series.
  F1418.F25 1984   327.7308   84-14634

ISBN 0-8447-3562-0
ISBN 0-8447-3563-9 (pbk.)

1 3 5 7 9 10 8 6 4 2

AEI Studies 409

Printed in the United States of America

Contents

Foreword

Since 1979 the American Enterprise Institute has been involved in a broad-gauged program of Latin American studies, exploring the main areas of convergence and conflict between the United States and its southern neighbors. During that time our Center for Hemispheric Studies has sponsored lectures, conferences, and working lunches with distinguished (and not yet distinguished) Latin Americans visiting Washington, as well as the publication of mongraphs, a series of occasional papers, and special issues of the *AEI Foreign Policy and Defense Review*.

When we entered this field some five years ago, our academic board made a conscious decision to expand the scope of AEI's traditional areas of research concern. We did so in the conviction that while economic issues remain important—indeed, vital—to international relations, they are never resolved in a political or cultural vacuum. Thus the task of scholarship in the service of policy is to map the larger framework in which decisions must be made and implemented.

Perhaps our most ambitious effort has been *Rift and Revolution: The Central American Imbroglio*, a collective study by thirteen scholars of the dimensions of conflict—both local and international—in what one journalist has called "the American Balkans." The editor of that volume, center director and AEI resident scholar Howard Wiarda, has taken some of the issues raised by it as the point of departure for a subsequent volume of his own, *In Search of Policy: The United States and Latin America*. There he examined our own foreign policy process with the same learning, objectivity, and good humor he has brought to bear in his well-known studies of the Dominican Republic, Portugal, and Latin America generally.

In *Rift and Revolution*, AEI resident fellow Mark Falcoff contributed a chapter entitled "The Apple of Discord: Central America in U.S. Domestic Politics," where he showed how events in the isthmus have had important backward linkages into the U.S. political system. In some ways he took what is called "dependency theory"—the dominant orthodoxy among academic Latin Americanists in the United States—and stood it on its head. He showed how, although U.S. eco-

i

nomic or security imperatives can weigh very heavily upon the small nations of Central America, in the end those imperatives are often thwarted or transformed in unexpected ways by the objects of policy themselves.

That is the theme to which he returns in these essays. Since they are case studies, they require a certain patience from the reader while each country's peculiar history (and involvement with the United States) is unraveled, detail by detail. They are unified, however, by one central theme: the way that relations between nations in the present era really operate, apart from (and often in opposition to) such evident power indicators as gross national product or the number and quality of their armed forces. By selecting some of the smallest and least powerful of American nations to make his point, Falcoff casts into bold relief one of the central problems of our time—the relationship between great powers and their clients, past and present. He does so in a way that is thoughtful, highly readable, and very timely. We take pleasure in bringing his findings to the attention of a wider reading public.

WILLIAM J. BAROODY, JR.
President
American Enterprise Institute

Preface

In the fiction of international law, all nations are created equal; in the real world of international politics, some nations are stronger and more influential than others. When the differences in power between one and another reach massive dimensions, the proper term for their bilateral relationship is asymmetry. For Latin American nations, this concept has long been—and for most it continues to be—the most useful in describing their relations with the United States. This is particularly true of the smaller countries, for which almost anything that Washington does or fails to do constitutes a policy of some sort—whether through a conscious decision or by mere inadvertence.

Asymmetries between nations are bound to produce frustrations and misunderstandings. They also engender legends. Almost every country south of the Rio Grande possesses a rich literature of conspiracy, in which virtually every untoward event in its history can be explained in terms of a grand design conceived in and implemented from U.S. centers of power. In itself such literature is almost invariably superficial and often harmless—an understandable attempt by small and sometimes humiliated nations to reflate their importance and find a more respectable place in the sun of universal history. But when, as has sometimes occurred in recent times, those legends are taken over and given a respectable place in the mainstream of American political debate, they become a serious matter of public policy. That is the point from which the essays in this book take their departure.

Their purpose is twofold. They seek to examine how asymmetries actually function in U.S.-Latin American relations, with special attention to the divergence between policies and their outcomes. This is important because the United States, uniquely among nations, expects its foreign policies to be an extension of its national values: good intentions count. If they are found lacking, nagging questions are raised about the fundamental decency of our leaders and institutions. But it is also important to understand how good intentions do not always suffice and to recognize soberly the limits of our power.

The other objective is to put an end to the promiscuous and irresponsible use of contemporary history. This, too, is of enormous moment because so much of what passes for foreign policy debate nowadays is nothing more than the stacking of defective metaphors against one another. The mere names of some countries—Vietnam, Chile—have come to evoke an entire theory of history. Yet few people have bothered to look closely at the facts upon which such enormous presumption rests. In this book I have purposely reopened several such cases and exhaustively reevaluated the evidence. I hope these exercises will help clear the air and promote a more dispassionate discussion of the role of the United States in the affairs of small countries and, by extension, what some are pleased to call the third world. As the title implies, the individual cases are small, but the stakes are not.

The studies in this book have been arranged to correspond to each of these priorities. I begin with Cuba because it was the first Caribbean nation to fall under a U.S. protectorate and because its relations with the United States have been the central obsession of all its governments since then. In some ways, indeed, the Castro revolution of 1959 was merely the culmination of many attempts to settle old scores with the United States, and the ambivalence that many Latin nations feel for Castro and his regime arises largely out of a "racial" sympathy for the trauma—real and imagined—provoked by U.S. occupation.

The chapter on Uruguay explores one of the primary consequences of the Cuban Revolution in South America—the growth of urban guerrilla warfare and newer forms of terrorism, response to which by the U.S. Agency for International Development (AID) has been the source of a highly controversial motion picture, *State of Siege*. By singling this film out for careful analysis, I intended to bring to light some of the major issues involved in a security relationship with a nation far from our borders and of arguably negligible military significance.

"Somoza, Sandino, and the United States" reopens the case of U.S. intervention in Nicaragua in the 1920s and 1930s, an event that, though extremely remote in time, has become the centerpiece of a national debate over our present posture toward the Sandinista regime, which came to power there in 1979. It takes pointed issue with some of the more conventional interpretations of the past U.S. role there and, in so doing, shows how historiography can shape (and misshape) public policy.

The study of external forces in the overthrow of President Salvador Allende in Chile (1970–1973) seems called for in light of the fact that it is the United States that stands condemned today—no less in the opinion of its own people than in that of the public worldwide—as the judge, jury, and executioner of the oldest democracy in South America. Since practically all of the subsequent restraints placed on the U.S. Central Intelligence Agency (CIA), particularly with reference to covert action, have arisen out of what Americans understand to have been its role in the Chilean tragedy, it seemed worthwhile to investigate the degree to which the evidence—in this case, the findings of a special legislative committee chaired by the late Senator Frank Church of Idaho—can fix American responsibility for events in that country.

Finally, the selection on El Salvador is added to provide a bit of methodological counterpoint: here is a case of Soviet, Cuban, and Nicaraguan involvement in a tiny country artfully denied by sources that would grant full faith and credit to virtually every shred of evidence if the United States were the nation in the dock. It also demonstrates that the United States is not the only power capable of making its influence felt—and meaningfully so—in the affairs of nations long thought to be within its traditional sphere of influence.

Most of these pieces have appeared in widely scattered academic journals over the past ten years but have nonetheless achieved a certain notoriety that justifies their republication. An exception is the final chapter on Chile, which appears in print for the first time. It is part of a larger study on the Allende period that will be published next year. I gratefully acknowledge the hospitality of the Hoover Institution on War, Revolution and Peace, Stanford University, where as a National Fellow in 1979–1980, I completed much of the research and writing.

1

The Cuban Revolution and the United States: A Longer Perspective

Few issues in U.S. foreign policy have provoked as much enduring controversy as our relations with revolutionary Cuba. Although the accumulated evidence is overwhelming that Fidel Castro consciously chose his country's destiny as an ally and pawn of the Soviet Union, a significant body of opinion in the United States—radiating from certain quarters of academe, the quality press, and the leftist clerisy—still assumes that the Cuban dictator was reluctantly forced into his present role by a blind, insensitive, ungenerous government in Washington. Since this sort of revisionism feeds on issues and needs that have only the slightest connection with the ostensible topic of discussion, it is not likely to go away. But the controversy itself is of more than historiographical or cultural interest. For from this view follows a clear policy corollary: that because U.S. hostility has failed to dissuade Castro from meddling in the troubled waters of the Caribbean, Central America, Africa, and the Middle East, perhaps it is time to try "normalizing" relations and negotiating our differences.

This idea has been around for some time, first advanced by the McGovernite wing of the Democratic party and eventually put to the test after 1977 through the opening of low-level diplomatic missions in both Washington and Havana. Although subsequent Cuban activities in Angola and the Horn of Africa led the Carter administration substantially to revise its estimates of Castro's intentions, the advocates of what might be called unconditional normalization remain unconvinced—and unrepentant. Confronted with the baldest evidence of continued Cuban adventurism, as in Central America, they either deny the accuracy of the data[1] or attempt to shift the blame back to the United States ("Cuba was forced to do what it did because of U.S. blunders and errors"). The most recent salvo in this campaign took the form of an article by Wayne Smith, recently retired chief of the U.S. mission in Havana, in which the Reagan administration was accused of willfully turning aside three Cuban offers in 1981 and 1982 to initiate substantive discussions of outstanding issues.[2]

Beneath this controversy lie two different ways to think about Cuba and therefore about U.S.-Cuban relations. One is to focus on the discrete disparities of power between the United States and Cuba, which necessarily emphasizes Cuba's relative weakness and vulnerability. This makes it possible to explain away Castro's conduct by his presumed perceptions of U.S. policy and exculpate Cuban actions by citing official U.S. rhetoric. From this perspective, Cuban policy is always seen as merely reactive, for which purpose it is necessary to play down the Soviet connection systematically, because that would suggest the existence of agendas far less amenable to U.S. rectification.

The other is to see the Cuban government as being launched upon a vast historic enterprise of its own, one that in the absence of external aid would be purely quixotic, to be sure, but that under the present circumstances is extremely dangerous to the security of the United States and its allies. Much liberal hand-wringing notwithstanding, this approach does not overemphasize Cuban subordination to Soviet purposes; rather, it takes the Cubans at their own word and, most seriously, purely on their own terms. It is also the only one that can offer any realistic suggestions for U.S.-Cuban policy in the future.

A Look Backward

Perhaps the most important fact about Cuba is that its relationship to the United States has been vastly different from that of any other Latin American country. Throughout the nineteenth century, while the island remained under Spanish control long after its sister nations had established their independence, various American statesmen— following a logic of geographical or strategic determinism—sought to acquire it through purchase or annexation. The idea of Cuba as an integral part of the United States was extraordinarily slow to die: as late as 1900 or 1901, after the United States had defeated Spain and occupied the island under a clear commitment to withdraw as expeditiously as possible, key figures in the U.S. military establishment and the government of occupation sturdily opposed the idea of self-determination. Eventually a compromise was reached: the United States opted to transfer authority to an elected government but forced the infant republic to recognize a "special relationship," embodied in a rider to an army appropriations bill known as the Platt amendment. This proviso, which the Cubans were compelled to carry over textually into their new constitution, conceded to the United States the right to intervene militarily and replace existing authority on the island whenever, in its sole opinion, "life, liberty, or property" appeared to be in peril.

Although the Platt amendment was finally abrogated by President Franklin D. Roosevelt in 1934, the overwhelming economic and strategic weight of the United States in Cuba remained so great that it was no exaggeration to say, as Ambassador Earl E. T. Smith (1955–1958) once did, that to the day of Castro's accession, the representative of the United States was the second most important man in the country, after the president. "And at times," he added in an unfortunate coda, "even more important than the President."

At the other end of this relationship, reactions were by no means unambiguous. Although the United States could not avoid acting in various ways as a goad to Cuban nationalism, it also constituted a strong pole of attraction. For much of the first half of the nineteenth century, for example, the prospect of annexation was as appealing to Cuba's planter class (fearful of Spanish abolitionist policies) as it was to U.S. expansionists or southern ideologues. Although the U.S. Civil War and the career of José Martí (1853–1895) did much to refocus energies on independence, some Cubans of importance right up to the American occupation still imagined that some form of absorption by the United States was inevitable, perhaps even ultimately desirable. One of these was the first president of the Cuban republic, Tomás Estrada Palma.

The idea of political union with the United States finally disappeared after the new structures were in place. But American economic influence, already very great in the sugar industry before Cuban independence, expanded thereafter to cover an astonishing range of activities—tobacco, minerals, transportation, banking, insurance, and, above all, a huge range of light industrial products. At issue was not merely geographic proximity or comparative advantage but decided consumer preference. Even now Cuban taste for things North American continues unabated, though in a somewhat different form. "Cuba wants to be a Communist country all right," a British scholar remarked after visiting the island in the early 1970s, "but it wants to be Communist in a very American way," citing the romance with pop art, films, skyscrapers, and—something that by then the United States had apparently gone on to lose—a naive worship of material progress for its own sake.

The observation itself speaks to an essential point: the U.S.-

Cuban relationship before 1959 could not be summed up in cold economic statistics; it always possessed a strong qualitative dimension. On one hand, Cubans have always considered the United States the principal point of reference for any evaluation of their own society. Hence, no matter how well the Cuban economy might have performed in comparison to that of other Caribbean nations or even to major republics of South America, it was not, after all, *those* economies with which Cuba compared itself. The mere presence of the United States ninety miles away holding up a model that perforce could never be fully replicated thus constituted a permanent force for the destabilization of Cuban politics. To the extent that the United States can negotiate past the walls Castro has erected around his people, this is still the case.

On the other hand, since the United States interfered so frequently in Cuban politics—first in 1898 and then, under the Platt amendment, in 1901, 1906–1909, 1921, and 1933—Cubans not unnaturally were led to blame Washington for all their country's shortcomings. That the purpose of these interventions might have been to restore financial integrity or ensure honest elections was quite beside the point, at least as far as Cubans were concerned, since in the end they brought neither. Instead, as a byproduct, these interventions generated a "second wave" of Cuban nationalism, which, in the words of one historian, often tended to lapse into "little more than a febrile, hysterical anti-Americanism." [3]

Cubans "Remembering" Their History

José Martí was a great visionary with a remarkable capacity to recast his dreams into unforgettable Spanish poetry and prose. His notion of a strong, independent Cuba, free of racial and economic distinctions, projecting its benevolent influence throughout the Caribbean basin and indeed the entire Spanish-speaking world, continued to haunt the island's intellectuals and reproach its politicians long after his death in the first days of the Second War of Independence (1895–1898). In fact, it was precisely his premature disappearance that gave life to his legend: he did not survive, as did so many leaders of the second and third rank, to be discredited by the actual practice of governing. Instead, reflecting upon the corruption, jobbery, and casual violence of Cuban politics, many succumbed to the notion, "If only Martí had lived . . ."

By the 1930s a sense of thwarted national destiny had come to overwhelm Cuban historical consciousness. A new generation of historians, whose outstanding figures were Emilio Roig de Leuschenring, Herminio Portell-Vilá, and Ramiro Guerra y Sánchez, began to argue in an extended form—in books, pamphlets, articles, and lectures—that Cuba had been diverted *ab initio* by the United States from the course that Martí and other patriots had outlined for it. They held, for example, that the United States had consistently opposed Cuban independence and had entered the war against Spain only after it had been essentially won by the Cuban patriot forces, or that, at any rate, General Shafter owed his victory at San Juan Hill to plans conceived by General Calixto García, or (more probably) that the American invasion force that won that battle could not have debarked successfully without the diversionary tactics of Cuban guerrillas. It was even suggested that corruption had been *introduced* into Cuban politics by the American intervention of 1906–1909, because the reigning proconsul, Judge Charles Magoon, had once been a machine politician in Chicago.

This irredentist mood, conceived in the 1920s when the first bloom of independence had worn off, grew to full maturity in the 1930s and 1940s, nourished by the continued frustrations of Cuban politics. The dictator Gerardo Machado was finally overthrown in 1933 after four years of struggle by politicians, students, and soldiers. But U.S. diplomacy, in the person of Ambassador Sumner Welles, undermined Machado's successor, Ramón Grau San Martín, in such a way that he was overthrown in March 1934, by Sergeant Fulgencio Batista. Logically, the United States was blamed for aborting Cuba's serious essay in populism, although when Grau and his protégé Carlos Prío Socarrás each took their turns at the presidency in 1944 and 1948, they proved very hollow prophets indeed; both regimes were notable for their cynicism and corruption, so much so, in fact, that many Cubans hailed the return of Batista in 1952.

Likewise, the U.S.–Cuban Reciprocity Treaty, signed with Batista's government in 1934, could be interpreted as an attempt to chain the island to monoculture and dependence on the U.S. market, although at the time the only alternative for the Cubans was to toss their unsalable sugar surpluses off the Havana wharf and starve. It was also the 1934 treaty that paved the way for the sugar quota, a portion of the U.S. domestic market (usually about 25 percent) automatically reserved for Cuban producers. Cuban nationalists often referred to the quota as a "yoke of imperialism," but when the Eisenhower administration chose to lift the yoke in 1960, Ché Guevara accused it of "economic aggression."

In this atmosphere of perpetual recrimination, no aspiring Cuban politician with serious ambitions could afford to appear less than an utterly uncompromising nationalist. But the economic and geographical realities of the day necessarily fixed limits on what could be done to lessen the island's dependence on the United States. This was the first lesson that every Cuban chief executive was obliged to learn. It explains why, on one hand, each was destined to disappoint his followers and, on the other, why until 1959 Cuban nationalists were still waiting for someone to pick up Martí's fallen banner. Put another way, as long as no Cuban leader was willing to ally his country with another great power, there was no way of effectively counterbalancing the predominance of the United States. But whatever the shortcomings of these men, they were serious patriots who had no desire to withdraw from one sphere of influence merely to enter another. The historical uniqueness of Fidel Castro consists precisely in the fact that he alone of Cuban leaders was sufficiently willing to sacrifice the relative welfare and independence of his country to settle its historical scores with the United States. Doing this exacted a price so high that all but the most left-wing (or opportunistic) of Cuban nationalists refused to accompany him.

Implications for U.S. Policy

This means that Castro's Cuba is a strange and volatile mixture of nationalism and communism. The nationalist component not merely dictates a proud rejection of the United States, which in itself would be understandable enough. It also informs an unconfessed desire for self-immolation, on one hand, and a messianic urge to project itself throughout Latin America and the world, on the other. These are, to be sure, very old themes in Cuban history. As Alistair Hennessy reminds us, the former can be found in the patriot armies of 1895, which were quite prepared to destroy the agricultural wealth of the island to expel the Spaniards. And Cuban nationalism under Martí was "always . . . couched in Latin American and universalist terms, not those of narrow Cubanism."[4] The sinister shadow of the first legacy fell over the missile crisis of 1962; that of the second continues to darken Cuban relations with the Puerto Rican terrorists, the Sandinistas in Nicaragua, and the violent left in El Salvador, not to mention parties, movements, and regimes halfway around the world.

The Communist component is too obvious to require elaboration. But under this heading the important point to grasp is that if Marxism-Leninism were the *only* feature of the Cuban regime, its inclination to export revolution would be seriously curtailed by the tasks of constructing "socialism in one island," striving, as it were, to become a sort of tropical Bulgaria. While there is considerable dispute over who is ultimately responsible for Cuba's failures over the past twenty years, no one but the most dogmatic Marxist ideologues have suggested that Castro's economy is some sort of advertisement for socialism. If all he wished to do were to convert the island into a Marxist economic system that actually worked, the full enormousness of that task alone would absorb every ounce of the Cuban dictator's energies—and keep him out of trouble elsewhere.

The reverse side of this coin is that if Castro were merely an intransigent Cuban nationalist or a die-hard Yankeephobe, he might create a few incidents at the United Nations or spend some unpleasant hours on the shortwave band, but he would be quite limited in his capacity to do much beyond this. For example, however one chooses to interpret Castro's intervention in Angola and the Horn of Africa—whether under pressure from the Kremlin or in support of a spurious "proletarian internationalism"—without Soviet logistical support the adventure would have remained, at best, a gleam in the Cuban dictator's eye. It is, after all, the capacity of the Soviets to give Castro a role on the larger stage of world politics that appeals to him and allows him to pervert what would otherwise necessarily be a more inward-looking, and for that reason more constructive, form of Cuban nationalism.

Unscrambling Cuban Messages

The past is thus an indispensable tool for the interpretation of Cuban foreign policy intentions in the present and future. The substance of these has not changed very much over the years and, on the surface, remains deceptively simple: Cuba has repeatedly offered to sit down and discuss with the United States their outstanding differences, once Washington agrees to do so "on a plane of equality." This sounds reasonable enough. The confusion arises when U.S. commentators imagine this to refer to a decent regard for Wilsonian notions of self-determination and the juridical equality of states. What the Cubans really mean by this statement is a recognition of their right to play a great power role, as if their foreign policy goals were due the same deference as those of the Soviet Union or China.

It is striking how many Americans who ought to know better miss this essential point. One is Wayne Smith, who faithfully records but does not quite know how to unscramble Cuban messages. Thus, in his version, the Cubans were *compelled* to intervene in Angola. Prior U.S. involvement there, he explains, threatened to bring about the defeat of the Popular Movement for the Liberation of Angola, and "the Soviets and the Cubans [could not] permit a cheap U.S. victory."[5] A similar logic informs his account of Cuban involvement in

Ethiopia. Having armed the Somalis, who then proceeded to mount an irredentist invasion of the Ogaden region, the United States (perhaps unintentionally) forced the Cubans to step in and aid their allies. In Central America, he adds, "Cuba will only stop supporting subversive groups if the United States also ceases to do so."[6]

The problem with these explanations is that they focus strictly on the formal-legal structure of international relations and utterly ignore the flesh-and-blood realities of geopolitics and international stratification. The harsh truth is that Cuba is simply not an important enough country in its own right to be *forced* to do anything outside its boundaries. It is certainly not the Soviet Union, although by combining the two ("The Soviets *and the Cubans* [could not] permit . . .") Smith cleverly obscures the point. Moreover, U.S. national interests simply cannot be treated on a "plane of equality" with Cuban aspirations—or fantasies. A case can certainly be made for the imperatives of great power or regional interests when they work to the benefit of the Soviet Union in given areas, such as Poland. Smith even understands them when they appear to favor the Soviets in Africa. It is not clear why he feels that similar concerns on the part of the United States are somehow out of line or, even more strangely, why Cuban agendas should be piggybacked onto those of more significant international actors.

A second difficulty arises when Cuban claims are taken at face value in a sort of inverse rendition of "my country, right or wrong." Insofar as these involve evaluations of U.S. actions, those actions are invariably inflated so as to make them seem grotesquely disproportionate. Here again Smith provides us with some invaluable examples. Between January and November 1981, he writes, the United States stepped up its "war of nerves" against Cuba, by which he means establishing Radio Martí, tightening the trade embargo, and "stimulating speculation that it might take military measures."[7] The Cubans then put 500,000 men under arms, strengthened military ties with Moscow, and bought "large quantities of arms" from the Soviets. "Surely," Smith writes, "the U.S. could not expect the Cubans to *disarm* in the face of U.S. threats."[8] In other words, the United States opens a radio station, cancels some tourist flights, and talks tough—while the Cubans arm to the teeth.

Now, one could easily argue that a foreign policy based on hollow threats alone is worse than none at all, but there is still a difference between words—no matter how intemperate—and actions. There is also a difference between actions of greater and lesser magnitude. Finally, to express concern over Cuban adventurism is not the same thing as asking the Cubans to disarm altogether, a request that has never been made by any U.S. government, as Smith is admirably equipped to know.

Or again, in December 1981, Smith writes, the "Cubans informed the United States that they had ceased shipping arms to Nicaragua, perhaps reflecting a softening of their own position in order to improve the atmosphere for negotiation."[9] Perhaps—but then again perhaps not. To be informed of something is not prima facie evidence that it has actually happened. The Cubans are well known for temporarily shutting off shipments to Central America so as to be able to claim publicly that they are not arming Nicaraguans or Salvadorans, which remains technically true—for that morning. Moreover, it would be quite possible to assemble a voluminous catalog of *post hoc* admissions by Castro that he had indeed shipped arms to Central America at given points in the past, which, when interpolated into the record, would prove that the Cuban dictator is a liar who confesses the truth—retroactively.

Likewise, in January 1981, after the failed "general offensive" of revolutionary forces in El Salvador, Smith reports that Cuban arms shipments to that country declined. "At the same time," he relates, "the Cubans signaled a desire for improved relations, and a disposition to exchange views [with the United States] on El Salvador."[10] This amounts to saying that in exchange for opening discussions (which, like U.S. "talks" with the North Koreans, could go on for infinity without resolving a single point of importance), the guerrillas in El Salvador could expect to receive 50 rifles a day instead of 100.

Further, one must really ask whether U.S. covert involvement in Ethiopia or Angola can be equated with the commitment of a major Cuban expeditionary force, one that, in fact, decisively turned the tables there in favor of the Soviets. One may also be permitted to doubt that U.S. assistance to "subversive groups" in Central America (presumably, anti-Sandinista forces operating on the Honduran-Nicaraguan border) can really be compared to the massive Cuban involvement not only in Nicaragua itself but throughout Central America and the Caribbean, leaving aside altogether the activities of thousands of Cuban security advisers in Africa and the Middle East.

Third, and finally, there is a tendency to confuse Cuban willingness to normalize relations with a readiness on Castro's part to revise his country's international role. As any diplomat will admit, the ordinary stuff of foreign affairs, taken on a day-to-day basis, is rather dull: consular matters, trade and sanitary regulations, drug enforcement, and so forth. In this undramatic mainstream, the Cubans would have no difficulty whatever functioning with the United States—indeed, one can think of all sorts of reasons why they might actually wish to, beginning with the fact that the Cuban economy is in very serious trouble. The Castro regime not only owes something approaching $9 billion to the Soviet Union and Eastern bloc countries but, what is surely more significant in the present context, has recently been compelled to request rescheduling of $3.4 billion in hard currency loans owed to Western trading partners and Japan. If economic relations with the United States were suddenly normalized, American bankers, who have performed so brilliantly in places like Poland, would be in a position to extend a lifeline of liquidity to one more failed socialist experiment.

But there is an important political dimension to all of this that must not be missed. The resumption of full economic relations between the United States and Cuba would summon to life once again an organized community of interest in Washington, New York, and elsewhere in the United States whose role would inevitably become that of advocating and defending Castro's policies. Functionally these people would play much the same role as the right-wing businessmen who before 1959 used to complain that the State Department and the American press were too hard on the dictator Batista. True, the personalities involved would be different; they would represent a different kind of economic community; they would employ different arguments; but the international implications of their role would also be different and more dangerous.[11]

There is also a bureaucratic dimension to diplomacy that makes simple formulas like "the resumption of discussions" or "the exchange of views" far more complicated and treacherous than might appear at first glance. Once negotiations begin, those involved acquire a vested interest in keeping them going, so that they cannot be said to have failed. That these negotiations might lead absolutely nowhere is the least of it: if, once discussions are under way, Castro decides to do something new and dramatic in Central America or elsewhere, he will be able to count upon an organized chorus within the State Department urging that no effective U.S. response be undertaken. ("Talks are under way, and we must do nothing to impair them.") Stylized shock and disappointment will resound through the editorial columns of the prestige press, and a new chapter in the black legend of American foreign policy will be born.

The truth is that a resumption of relations with the United States under circumstances that succeeded in separating international issues from all other matters has *always* appealed to Castro. Smith interprets this as a healthy sign of Cuban pragmatism,[12] as if it were some sort of favor to the United States, when in fact it would simply permit the Cuban dictator to reduce the domestic costs of Cuba's great power role. Even today Castro is enough of a nationalist to want to reduce Cuba's heavy economic dependence on the Soviet Union, all the more so because the Soviets have at given times and places used their influence to restrain him from some of his more bizarre projects. It may also be that Castro feels he should have a greater voice within the councils of Soviet communism in deciding precisely which revolutionary theaters should receive priority in the dispatch of Cuban soldiers and intelligence operatives. This would obviously be easier if he could locate a new source of economic leverage. Whether the United States might wish to provide it is quite another matter.

A Long Wait

That Cuba would benefit from a normalization of relations with the United States cannot be doubted; it is far less clear, however, what advantages would accrue to the other party. For if the past twenty years have established that it is perfectly possible for a small Latin American country—under very special circumstances—to defy the United States and live to tell about it, they have also proved that the United States can live without Cuban sugar, tobacco, rum, winter vegetables, beaches, and tourist hotels. In fact, the only thing that Cuba has that the United States could really use is the one thing it cannot now offer—an admission, however tacit, that the island's ambitions have far outrun its capabilities and that the nationalist revolution has pursued its goals so blindly and intransigently as to become almost a negation of itself. To make that statement would require a separation of one of the two central strands that have made up Cuban policy since the revolution, and as long as Castro is alive and in control of events, this is not at all likely. Hence, U.S. diplomacy must settle in for a long wait.

This is a counsel that will dissatisfy many. For in foreign relations as in much else, Americans are a practical people in a hurry to get things done. How often we seem to say, "Let us deal with the concrete issues, so that we can move on to the bright, sunny uplands of aid and trade, tourism, and scientific exchanges." The fact that other societies might prefer to make ancient grudges or *folies de grandeur* the stuff of their foreign policy makes no sense to us, and therefore we refuse to take those attitudes seriously. When our excessive pragmatism fails to engage the unwilling partner, we slump into doubt and despair, asking ourselves what *we* have done wrong.

Such notions betray an ethnocentrism of the highest order—curious because it is practiced here by people who could normally be expected to regard the view of other nations as equal in value (if not

11

indeed superior in wisdom) to those of our own. For whatever reason, in the Cuban case they have forgotten that other nations have other memories. If they cannot turn history around and make it end differently, they certainly have no obligation to make life any easier for the victor.

Undoubtedly someday the United States will want to resume full diplomatic relations with Cuba. But before that can happen, the Cubans themselves will have to rethink the meaning of their national experience, much as the Chinese seem to have done. They can be helped to do this, but no one can finish the job for them. And there is no point in pretending that honeyed words to gullible (or alienated) Americans will ever replace the aerial photograph as the truest indicator of Cuban intentions.

Notes

1. See chapter 3, "El Salvador: The U.S. White Paper Reexamined."
2. Wayne Smith, "Dateline Havana: Myopic Diplomacy," *Foreign Policy*, no. 48 (Fall 1982), pp. 158–74.
3. C. A. M. Hennessy, "The Roots of Cuban Nationalism," in R. F. Smith, ed., *Background to Revolution: The Development of Modern Cuba*, 2d ed. (New York: Huntington, 1979), p. 28.
4. Ibid.
5. Smith, "Dateline Havana," p. 170.
6. Ibid., p. 174.
7. Ibid., p. 163.
8. Ibid., p. 164 (emphasis added).
9. Ibid., p. 166.
10. Ibid., pp. 160–61.
11. For a preview, see Irving Louis Horowitz, "The Cuba Lobby: Supplying Rope to a Mortgaged Revolution," in Irving Louis Horowitz, ed., *Cuban Communism*, 4th ed. (New Brunswick, N.J.: Transaction, 1981), pp. 505–27.
12. Smith, "Dateline Havana," p. 171.

2
Uruguay: The Tupamaros on the Silver Screen

The French writer Paul Nizan once remarked that the diplomatic correspondent was the historian of the present. Perhaps a generation or so ago that was still true; in the contemporary period the honor has passed in the industrial countries to television and in Latin America to the novel and especially to motion pictures. The cinema is a late-blooming Latin American art form and bears all the marks of its recent emergence. Since in many cases it follows rather than precedes the advent of television—in marked contrast to Europe and the United States—it has rapidly developed a style that might be called "documentary": to speak here of a "social" or "political" cinema is nearly redundant, for clearly all *important* Latin American films are about politics. For one thing, in many of the republics there is simply nothing else for intellectuals to talk about; for another, no single aspect of life capsulizes the tensions generated by underdevelopment so much as the political scene; for yet another, almost no other kind of film stands a chance in a highly competitive export market.

The same rules apply to outsiders when they approach the region with a motion picture camera. Since for the inhabitants of the North Atlantic countries the abstractions "Latin America," "unrest," and "revolution" are all one and the same thing, many foreign film makers find it difficult to imagine nonpolitical themes for productions set south of the U.S. border.[1] And when the *cinéaste* in question is a European, particularly one with leftist leanings and intellectual pretensions, the film habitually depicts the grim reality of U.S. imperialism, not only because it is good box office in Paris and Milan (and now in New York and Iowa City) but also because, for an extraordinary number of Europeans (and a growing host of Americans), "Latin America" has no internal life of its own, a life rich in contradictions and conflict, but rather survives as a kind of picturesque extension of the U.S. Department of State, the Central Intelligence Agency, and

Originally published under the title "The Uruguay That Never Was: A Historian Looks at Costa-Gavras's *State of Siege*," *Journal of Latin American Lore*, vol. 2, no. 2 (Winter 1976), pp. 239–56. Reprinted with permission of the Regents of the University of California.

the United Fruit Company. Such, at any rate, is the Latin America—
and specifically the Uruguay—that provides the setting for Constantin Costa-Gavras's political thriller *State of Siege* (1973).

State of Siege: **Documentary?**

Created by the director of *Z* and *The Confession* and written by Franco
Solinas (*The Battle of Algiers, Burn!*), *State of Siege* has enjoyed an
international success. Although it was banned in Brazil, Uruguay,
and Chile (by *both* Allende and the junta), it broke all records for a
first-week run when it opened in Buenos Aires in August 1973. Its
commercial success in the United States has been somewhat limited
(owing in part to the barbarously dubbed English version), but it
continues to enjoy wide and continuous exhibition on American university campuses; in Europe, especially in France, where it requires
no subtitles, it has become a contemporary film classic.

This is so—let it be said immediately—not merely because Costa-
Gavras and Solinas have successfully exploited so many misconcep-
tions and prejudices about Latin America: *State of Siege* is excellent
entertainment. Filmed in Chile with an international cast, marvel-
ously photographed and edited, it uses authentic settings and human
types to the point that it can be said that here, practically for the first
time, southern South America appears on the screen as it really "is."
At the same time, *State of Siege* fully exploits the rich dramatic possibilities inherent in a crime of international consequence, the kidnapping by leftist guerrillas of an American police expert on loan to a
South American government. The structure of the film calls for the
parallel development of two themes: the frantic search by the local
government—unpopular and under strong harassment from both left
and right—for the victim, it hopes unharmed; and the simultaneous
attempt by the guerrillas to negotiate the release of all political prisoners through an exchange. These two lines are periodically intersected by flashbacks on the life of the American agent, which in their
totality provide not only a background to the kidnapping but a moral
justification for the execution that follows. Although Costa-Gavras
and Solinas reveal the "ending" in the first few minutes, it is a tribute
to their cinematic skill that they are nonetheless capable of generating
the kind of tension normally associated with the conventional sus-
pense film. Finally, and perhaps here I merely express a personal
preference, *State of Siege* affords the irresistible fascination of witness-
ing history close up: at the U.S. embassy and in the Ministry of
Interior; at the university and in the Chamber of Deputies; in the
State Department and at the national palace—and in the eye of the

storm, the "people's prison," where the sole object of a national dragnet is being held. Above all, there is the sense of traveling to a far country, underscored by the wonderfully gothic quality of the physical settings, particularly the national palace and the university. There archaic windows and doors, illuminated by a dull, gray backlight, are flanked by Second Empire furniture and draperies. Their musty textures depict, in an apparently uncontrived but unmistakable manner, the decadence not only of a government but of an entire way of life.

Had the creators of so fascinating a motion picture been willing to recognize a clear boundary between art and life, there would be little reason to quibble over the actual historical details upon which it is based. But since they have so unambiguously claimed for their film all the prerogatives of a documentary, they must allow their work to be judged by the canons that normally apply to that genre.[2] What follow, then, are a series of caveats that occurred to me after a third viewing of *State of Siege* and subsequent study of the script and the accompanying published materials. They are inspired, and I hope informed, by a long acquaintance with Uruguay and by residence in Montevideo and Buenos Aires during the period depicted in the motion picture. These observations do not, of course, qualify as film criticism except in the broadest sense of the term. They are, rather, an attempt at intelligent commentary by an observer and student of the "reality" that *State of Siege* pretends to replicate.

Factual Background of the Film

Before I begin, however, it might be useful to review some of the actual events that form the background of the film. On July 31, 1970, partisans of the Uruguayan Movimiento de Liberación Nacional (MLN), also known as Tupamaros, simultaneously abducted from their homes in Montevideo American police adviser Dan Mitrione and Brazilian Consul Aloysio Mares Dias Gomide. Two other intended targets, Michael Jones, second secretary of the U.S. embassy, and Nathan Rosenfeld, U.S. cultural attaché, managed to evade their captors and escape. As was customary, the purpose of the kidnappings was eminently political—to secure the release of a number of leftist and trade union leaders jailed by the government. When President Jorge Pacheco Areco vehemently refused to bargain with the kidnappers, on August 7 they abducted American agronomist Claude Fly of the Agency for International Development (AID). And at almost the same time a manhunt virtually without precedent in Uruguayan history yielded some sixty suspected Tupamaros, including the lawyer Raúl Sendic, generally believed to be the founder of the

15

group. On August 9, their sense of urgency increased, the MLN announced that unless all political prisoners were set free, Mitrione would be executed. After hurried consultation with Washington, the Uruguayan government reiterated its refusal, and a few hours thereafter the corpse of Mitrione was found stuffed into a 1948 Chevrolet convertible parked in a suburb of Montevideo. Dias Gomide and Fly were released unharmed some months later.

Except for the return of Dias Gomide and Fly, all these events are depicted in the film more or less in the order in which they occurred. Only the names are changed—or omitted altogether. Mitrione becomes Philip M. Santore (pronounced, in the American manner, Santor); Claude Fly becomes Mr. Snow; Dias Gomide becomes Fernando Campos B.; and Jones and Rosenfeld are metamorphosed into Anthony Lee, second secretary of the U.S. embassy. One figure is apparently fictitious—Carlos Ducas, an elderly journalist whose inexhaustible energy and tenacious curiosity eventually unearth the true nature of Santore and his mission within the country. I say "apparently fictitious" because Ducas is obviously modeled closely on Carlos Quijano, publisher of the left-wing intellectual weekly *Marcha*.

Portrayal of Mitrione

Alas, to depict events faithfully "as they happened" does not amount to explaining or interpreting them properly. This is preeminently the case in the miscast portrayal of Mitrione/Santore by the distinguished French actor Yves Montand. The script calls for something more than a transplanted Indiana cop; at all events, Santore resembles no American policeman I have ever met or heard about. To start with, Santore possesses a kind of Satanic elegance: as the script indicates, he is "dressed in a dark, well-cut suit"; his face "shows little emotion; he is obviously in control of himself."[3] He lives in a house in Montevideo that "resembles a home in any American town,"[4] which is possible only if the town in question is Montecito, California, or Palm Beach, Florida. Above all, he is endowed with a kind of dialectical skill that is at least the equal, and at times the superior, of that possessed by his captors, who after all are supposed to be Marxists.

> SANTORE. I don't meddle in politics. . . . I'm a technician. . . . There might appear to be some contradictions. But . . . I'm a traffic and communications technician, and the problems are the same whether you're dealing with a democracy or a dictatorship.[5]

HUGO (Tupamaro interrogator). And the Brazilian bishops who denounced the tortures, are they Communists too?
SANTORE. Who knows?[6]

SANTORE. Our task [in the Dominican Republic, 1965–1966] was to reorganize the police force and to restore order.
HUGO. What type of order, Mr. Santore?
SANTORE. Civil order! Which is the opposite of chaos, theft, and looting.
HUGO. You must mean the order of the United Fruit Co., don't you? And the role of the other Yankee companies in Latin America?[7]

On one hand, Santore is a kind of police ideologist, a worthy companion of Victor Hugo's Javert. "Governments come and go," he declares in one of the pithier statements in the film; "the police remain."[8]

HUGO. You belong to a special breed?
SANTORE. You might say so, yes. . . . We're cut out for law and order, which means we don't care much for change. We're conservatives.
HUGO. Here a lot of people turn cop because they're hungry, not because they're cut out for it.
SANTORE. Yes, but they join the police force. While others, if they're hungry, turn into thieves.
HUGO. You think hunger leaves a man a choice?
SANTORE. I think a man, a *real* man, always chooses.[9]

On the other hand, he is a highly polished cold war dialectician, who sounds as if he spent most of his spare time reading Gerhart Niemeyer, Stefan Possony, and Robert Strausz-Hupé, and perhaps (strictly for methodological purposes) Maurice Merleau-Ponty.

HUGO. You say you're defending freedom and democracy. . . . Your methods are war, fascism, and torture. . . . Surely you agree with me, Mr. Santore?
SANTORE. You are subversives, Communists. You want to destroy the foundations of our society, the fundamental values of Christian civilization, the very existence of the free world. You are an enemy who must be fought in every possible way.
HUGO. I don't think we have anything more to say to each other.
SANTORE. I don't either.[10]

SANTORE (to ESTE, another Tupamaro interrogator). As for you, you have no choice. If you kill me, it will be an act of cruelty and impotence. If you don't kill me, it will be a proof of weakness, thus of impotence.[11]

Anything being possible, one cannot say that such a policeman, even such an American policeman, might not exist; although it requires an enormous stretch of the imagination, perhaps he might find his way into the overseas operations of AID. And pushing the matter to its ultimate extreme, perhaps he might even land in Uruguay. But he would not resemble the real Dan Mitrione in the slightest. This we know because the Tupamaros published their interrogations of Mitrione after his death, and those dialogues were fully available to Costa-Gavras and Solinas, who claim that they recast them for dramatic purposes but that they remain "faithful to the spirit of his character and [that] of the Tupamaros."[12] Here are some selections; let the reader decide.

MITRIONE. . . . let me say this, I hope you get the problems solved before you have to kill any more on either side. That doesn't accomplish anything, really.

TUPAMARO. Ah, we hope it too, but we don't see it very soon.

MITRIONE. I hope so. Miracles have happened before. The thing I say is that the Tupamaros . . . are not people from Mars. You are all Uruguayans . . . that want to see your government do things, what you consider better, because it isn't a case like in the United States, where we do have a very definite separation between the black and the white.

TUPAMARO. That's a pretty rough problem, isn't it?

MITRIONE. Oh yes, my goodness, it is a rough problem. But here you don't have that. Everybody is an Uruguayan, but the philosophy and the ideology is different, that's all.

TUPAMARO. Yes, and it's pretty hard to do it without violence, you know. I've been trying for long before I decided to work with violence, you know. I didn't care about my life, I cared about hunger and exploitation.

MITRIONE. I'm strictly at your mercy, really. And I understand that. . . . Well, the only thing I regret about all this: I don't like one thing and that is that too many innocent people suffer. My wife and children, there is no reason for them to be suffering.

TUPAMARO. I have a wife and children too, but you know, you do it for money and I don't. You choose your work

18

and the States choose a political way to do things and you are engaged with your country and so you are under your own law.

MITRIONE. Yeah.

TUPAMARO. I am sorry about them too. I am sorry about other families of all friends who are in prison being tortured or killed. There are many really, many innocent people have to suffer. But do you know about one million boys and girls under five years die every year in Latin America?

MITRIONE. Of hunger?

TUPAMARO. Yes sir, and that is not a way of control, birth control, you know. And how do you feel about other guerrilla movements. You know that we don't work all the same way. You have seen that.

MITRIONE. Well, every one of them has to work according to his surroundings. What everyone can work best. From what I have read, I think that the Tupamaros are a little bit smarter than some of the others, because Tupamaros don't kill unless they have to. I think the others indiscriminately kill. I think they shoot and ask questions later. . . .

TUPAMARO. What do you think is going to happen with all Latin America?

MITRIONE. Well, Latin America is going to be all right. I don't care, I don't know how long it is going to take, but there are people who love life, there are people in every country who love life. Governments have problems, but some day it's going to be solved, you mark my words.

TUPAMARO. Yes.

MITRIONE. It's going to be solved. All these buildings and all these stores and all these schools and all these football fields are not accidents. They were built by intelligent people. They are not going to be destroyed overnight.

TUMPAMARO. No, we hope not.

MITRIONE. No, I know they are not. It's just going to be a case of how long it is going to take. Some countries will take longer than others.[13]

Now, there is no point in claiming that Mitrione was a political innocent. Attached to the published version of the script is a summary of his activities provided by "Police Inspector X," which claims that while "advising" the Uruguayan security forces his innovations included the establishment of a spy underground in high schools to assemble dossiers on rebellious student leaders, the placing of hidden cameras at Carrasco International Airport to photograph persons leaving for socialist countries, the use of *agents provocateurs* to discredit and confuse left-wing movements, the introduction of explosives for political purposes, and so on. Since Inspector X remains anonymous, there is no way of establishing the veracity of his allegations. But at the very least, we might hazard the judgment that Mitrione was a man engaged in dangerous, highly paid work that, whatever its official cover, amounted to deep involvement in the political affairs of the Uruguayan state. He was not a humanitarian, and he was not engaged in the reestablishment of "law and order" in the conventional sense (although that fact was determined as much as anything else by preexisting Uruguayan conditions). But neither was he the elegant police ideologist cum cold war intellectual represented by Philip M. Santore. Rather, he was something more and less than this: he was—if Inspector X is to be believed, that is—a brutal and ruthless American policeman whose authoritarian impulses simply got out of control in an environment in which he was subject to few restrictions and in which the "enemy" professed the (to him) supreme heresy of Marxism and appeared capable of effectively subverting the government, perhaps of bringing it down altogether. The difference is important: Montand conceives the character he plays as "a perfectly respectable man . . . [sharing] certain parallel[s] with a convinced Stalinist . . . a man on the Right who is equally convinced of his own righteousness."[14] But this merely makes Santore a tragic, possibly even a heroic, figure, depending merely on the ideological predisposition of the audience.[15] The real Mitrione lacked Santore's precise if amoral calculus of means and ends, and he filtered the world around him through an ideological prism that was extraordinarily distorted in its refractions. In the "people's prison" he was by turns frightened, cowardly, and morose and at times obsequious to his captors. But Costa-Gavras and Solinas cannot allow that his was the banality of evil, for that would amount to admitting that Americans are not ten feet tall, that their operatives can be contemptible rather than fearsome, and, above all, that their intelligence and espionage apparatus is not the omnipotent force in Latin America (and elsewhere) that their conspiratorial imagination requires.[16]

Relations between the United States and Uruguay

This last point is important as well, for to explain the nature, origins, and purpose of Mitrione's activities, Costa-Gavras and Solinas find it necessary to explore the larger relationship between the United States and Uruguay. Here, too, the result is something less than successful. As defined early in the film, the motive force of U.S. policy is economic.

> DUCAS (to the representative of AID). Whether it's by drinking beer, swallowing aspirin, brushing his teeth, cooking in an aluminum pan, using a refrigerator, or heating a room . . . every day, each citizen of my country contributes to the development of your economy. This contribution takes on full significance when we enter the military sphere. [From gunshot to cannonshot, from mere jeep to tank or plane, our economy contributes to maintaining your armaments monopoly.][17]

As members of the cabinet pass from their limousines to the presidential palace, Ducas reviews their extensive economic connections, especially with American firms. Thus we are told that the minister of economy is president of four corporations, two of them American, the minister of foreign affairs represents the Rockefeller group in Uruguay, and the influential Clan Herbert heads seven corporations, three of them American. The evidence is clear: the United States, possessing a strong economic stake in Uruguay, cannot afford to be indifferent to its political life.

Unfortunately such crude economic determinism generates far more heat than light. In the first place, Uruguay has not for many years been a particularly golden field of investment for U.S. overseas capital or for investment from any other foreign or domestic source.[18] This is due not to the instability of its political life, which is relatively recent, but rather to a series of reforms dating back to World War I, which established a mixed economy. As one U.S. government publication characterized that economy in 1970, "Most sectors [are] effectively controlled by the State, either directly or through public agencies: [The] State [is] also engaged in industrial and commercial activities, in some cases as a monopoly and in others in partnership with private companies."[19] I infer here not that Uruguay possesses a socialist economic system in the full sense of the term but rather that at the time of the Mitrione affair it was a South American welfare state, possessing a correspondingly large administrative structure and an oversized bureaucracy, which frequently made the principal companies (such as PLUNA, the state airline, or the Frigorífico Nacional, the state meatpacking house) unprofitable from a strictly economic point of view.

Accurate and up-to-date figures on investment in Uruguay by the United States (or by any other country, for that matter) are extraordinarily hard to come by, but we do know that most of the major American concerns in southern South America have preferred to base their operations in either Argentina or Brazil, except for IBM, SUD-AMETEX (a big textile firm), and a General Motors distributorship. This is not surprising, given Uruguay's economic geography. Its population of about 3 million is too small to support a large domestic market for finished goods, and it lives largely through the export of agricultural staples (which earn 97 percent of the country's foreign exchange). Wool accounts for approximately half these staples, beef and arable crops the remainder. The principal production units for export agriculture are sheep and cattle *estancias*, owned and operated by Uruguayans and in a few cases by Argentines and Brazilians. Such American concerns as the King Ranch, which recently bought land in the Argentine province of Corrientes to develop a new breed of cattle, are conspicuously absent from Uruguay. Nor is the pattern of its foreign trade one that would imply a crushing dependence on the United States. The figures in table 2–1 reveal a pattern of foreign trade relations remarkably diverse for a Latin American country.

These figures do not, of course, tell the entire story. Uruguay is bound to the United States in a variety of ways not reflected in trade

TABLE 2–1
PATTERN OF URUGUAY'S FOREIGN TRADE, 1968

Sources of Imports		Destination of Exports	
Country or area	Percentage of total	Country or area	Percentage of total
United States	22.5	United States	12.1
Latin America	30.4	Latin America	11.1
EUROCOM [a]	17.4	EUROCOM [a]	26.7
Great Britain	4.6	Great Britain	21.1
Rest of EFTA [b]	6.6	Rest of EFTA [b]	4.2
Rest of Western Europe	0.6	Rest of Western Europe	13.3
Eastern Europe	0.4	Eastern Europe	4.0
Asia [c]	13.4	Asia	7.0
Oceania	1.6	Oceania	0.4
Africa	2.5	Africa	0.1

a. EUROCOM = the Common Market or European Community.
b. European Free Trade Association.
c. Includes Kuwait, from which Uruguay bought considerable amounts of petroleum.

SOURCE: Adapted from Instituto de Economía (FCEA), Universidad de la República, *Uruguay, estadísticas básicas* (Montevideo, 1969), pp. 72, 76.

statistics. It is a party to U.S.-sponsored hemispheric defense treaties; it receives from the United States military missions, technical aid, surplus foods, Fulbright professors and students, Peace Corps volunteers, Walt Disney films, and the Spanish version of *Reader's Digest*. Probably many of the replacement parts for its industrial machinery, much of its new technology, and some vital raw materials are of North American origin. And it would be naive indeed to suppose that because of a lack of direct U.S. investment or a predominantly European orientation to foreign trade, the United States is without influence in Uruguay. But following the logic at least partly outlined in *State of Siege*, Mitrione might as well have been a German, an Englishman—possibly even a Kuwaiti. Yet of course we know this is unlikely. The reason is cleverly glossed over by the film: namely, that the principal motives of U.S. policy in Uruguay are ideological and strategic. (There can be no mistaking the scenarist's intention, since he makes the same error when referring to the Dominican Republic and the United Fruit Company.) Yet nothing else so successfully explains the intransigence of the U.S. government on this issue as the lack of a major economic referent. Had there been a significant American investment community in Uruguay, its leaders might well have urged a conciliatory policy upon Washington, judging by the way other such communities have acted in the past toward Latin American regimes fundamentally friendly to their interests.[20] In such a case, the United States might well have acted just as Ducas (erroneously) predicts in the film that it will act, namely, to "compel the President [of Uruguay] and the government . . . to accept the exchange and release of all the political prisoners.[21] Instead, the United States opted to fight the matter out to the bitter end, conscious of the irreparable damage it would inflict upon the fabric of Uruguayan political life and mindful of the inevitable sentence of death it would visit upon one of its valued and trusted agents. The reason, we repeat, was fundamentally political. On one hand, the kidnapping of Mitrione threatened to reveal how easily a handful of determined partisans could humiliate the security forces of a Latin American government and render it utterly incapable of protecting foreign residents. On the other, it presented Washington with the specter of an entirely new (and possibly successful) revolutionary strategy—urban guerrilla warfare. Given Latin America's vast and rapidly growing urban population, this strategy seemed to offer far greater opportunities for social rebellion (if not revolution) than those afforded by the Castro model of a peasant-based insurgency, a model that had been tried throughout the 1960s in many countries and found wanting.

Finally, as in much of its history, Uruguay may have been a

victim of geography. Sandwiched between the two colossi of the south, Argentina and Brazil, it could not be allowed (from Washington's point of view) to degenerate into chaos or revolution, for fear of the contagion's spreading to contiguous areas where the United States (and other investing countries) really do possess important economic as well as political interests.

Uruguay: Allegory for Latin America?

Doubtless some would rush to defend the film on the grounds that this critique has been too literal, contending that whatever the facts may be, Uruguay has merely been used as a convenient allegory for Latin America. Thus Solinas declared in an interview that "for us, the general theme of the processes of imperialism was more important than the history of a single country." To which Costa-Gavras added, "Of course, Uruguay is not the main character. It is the background, the environment to which our 'character' comes and in which he plays his part and dies."[22] *The problem is that the film makers go out of their way to establish a purely Uruguayan locale.* Portraits of Artigas grace every government office; the seal of the republic appears on the ministries and on the desk of the president as he addresses the nation on television; the police are dispatched to Pocitos, Plaza Garibaldi, El Cerro, La Rambla—actual districts of Montevideo; the airport is clearly identified as Carrasco. Had the makers of *State of Siege* wished to enhance its Latin American setting, they certainly could have omitted these and other details, all the more so since the film was actually made in Chile. Instead, they wished to "document" Uruguay and have it stand at the same time for Latin America as a whole. The result is a distortion of two realities instead of one.

Just how Costa-Gavras and Solinas might have depicted Latin America if they had set out to do so is difficult to say, for in their view the sinister hand of the United States determines virtually every aspect of the region's political, economic, and cultural life. In the most revealing statement of the interview previously cited, Solinas frankly avows that "from a political point of view, the basic problem of our epoch is actually the role of the policeman which the United States plays in the entire world." Concretely, in the case of his native Italy, we are told that "each time there is an attempt to stop the advance of the broad masses of the people, it is always supported by the U.S. through the usual diplomatic channels, through NATO, the secret services, the machinations and provocations organized directly or through intermediaries." Costa-Gavras chimes in that "to take apart and explain this mechanism in Latin America, Vietnam, or Europe is in effect the same thing."[23] Anyone who can believe that the intervention of the United States is the major reason why Italy does not now have a Marxist government can surely convince himself that the same holds true for Latin America. For if the industrialists of Milan, the urban bourgeoisie, the Catholic church, the conservative (if benighted) peasantry, and the Mafia can all be ignored by an Italian, how much easier it must be for him to pretend that in Latin America there are virtually no authentic national interests favoring the preservation of the status quo.

Curiously enough, this interpretation is sometimes regarded as convenient by certain kinds of Latin American conservatives, particularly those charged with the unlovely task of shoring up the established order through force and violence. Costa-Gavras tells us that a few days after Mitrione's kidnapping, Alejandro Otero, the police commissioner in charge of the information bureau, told a Brazilian journalist that "it was Mitrione who introduced systematic torture into Uruguay."[24] We have no way of knowing whether the good commissioner winked at the newsman when he said this or whether the latter wrote up the matter tongue in cheek. Nor can we properly evaluate the claim by an "unidentified police commissioner" (what a passion for anonymity these men have!) that Mitrione brought an "electrode torture device" to Uruguay in his diplomatic bags. Nor can we know what relationship exists—if any—between the arrival of Mitrione in Montevideo and the report of an investigative commission in the Uruguayan parliament that "in the last several months [of 1969–1970], with political prisoners, the use of torture had become systematic."[25] On such shaky and inconclusive evidence, Costa-Gavras and Solinas rush in to make the electrode torture story the *pièce de résistance* of their case against Mitrione. First, in a horrifying sequence set somewhere in Brazil, Santore's policemen-students are "instructed" in the use of the device—on a live subject, of course. Then in rapid succession we see him arrive to take up his post in the Dominican Republic, then Uruguay. On both occasions he steps off the plane with his wife, his children, and his macabre cargo marked "diplomatic baggage." Then, just to make sure we get the point, we see him bring the bags into a restricted section of police headquarters in Montevideo. In the presence of his highest-ranking colleagues, they are opened; the contents provoke the same response as that of a child receiving a long-dreamed-of toy for Christmas. In the end, even Santore alludes indirectly to his guilt, for when left alone with his fellow captive, Consul Campos, the following dialogue takes place.

CAMPOS. What could they possibly have against me?

SANTORE. Maybe not against you.
CAMPOS. Against whom, then?
SANTORE. Your government.
CAMPOS (silent for a moment, incredulous). Hold what
against my government?
SANTORE. The tortures, for instance.[26]

Now the International Police Academy is not precisely a training
school for liberalism, but it is extremely doubtful that the use of
electrode torture devices (or the techniques of torture in general)
figure in the curriculum, either in Washington or in Latin America.
And the reason is singularly depressing: the use of torture in political
interrogations is today a regrettably international practice, recogniz-
ing no ideological boundaries and requiring a minimum of technology and practically no instruction whatever. In some countries it
assumes a more violent or harmful aspect than in others, depending
on the degree of political stability, the traditions of democratic government (or absence of them), civilian control of the police, and so
on.[27] One supposes, in other words, that policemen possess an innate
desire to use, shall we say, forceful methods of interrogation, a drive
that under normal circumstances and in the context of democratic
government can be kept adequately (though, one imagines, never
completely) under control. But when a civilian government is humiliated by terrorists and faced with a national and international crisis of
confidence (not to mention a serious economic slump), it can assert
but little control over the conduct of its own security forces. This was
preeminently the case in Uruguay, where in 1970 a long-established
constitutional order notable for its commitment to the rule of law was
in crisis. That crisis had its origins in a drastic drop in the world price
of wool, in a general economic stagnation, in the exhaustion of political ideas and the decadence of established political parties—but also
in the promiscuous use of violence by the "romantic" left. (Just how
far the Tupamaros advanced the cause of sadism at police headquarters by abducting Mitrione and Dias Gomide will never be known.)
   My intent here is not to deny the existence of tortures or to
absolve Mitrione from personal blame for whatever activities he may
have become involved in, still less to excuse the United States government for fishing—however much or little—in the troubled waters of
Uruguayan politics. But how ironic it is that two European film
makers—and left-wing ones at that—should come to pardon the Uruguayan establishment for its failures in the economic field by blaming
U.S. "imperialism" or (even indirectly) to exempt from blame the
Uruguayan police by accepting, even partly, its whining alibis when

caught literally red-handed in the torture chambers. For, clearly, to believe that they knew only occasionally the arts of "forceful interrogation" before Dan Mitrione got off the plane at Carrasco airport is to ask for a monumental—one might say almost biblical—suspension of doubt.[28]

In part, of course, the problem is that Costa-Gavras and Solinas are not interested in Uruguay as such, as we have seen. Yet there must have been some second thoughts after the production was complete, for Solinas suggests rather wistfully that "it is perhaps regrettable that the 1968 period, this moment of the evolution of the country's traditional order, does not appear in the film."[29] Regrettable indeed, for it might explain a great deal, though not necessarily from the desired ideological perspective.

Recent Events in Uruguay

Once again, let us refer to some aspects of recent Uruguayan history. For all but 9 of the last 114 years, Uruguay has been ruled by the Colorado party, whose traditional base of power has been (at least in recent times) the middle and working classes of Montevideo. It was this party, through its most significant historical persona, President José Battle y Ordóñez (1903–1907; 1911–1915), that established during the first two decades of this century the apparatus of a secular, democratic welfare state. By 1958 a worsening economic situation encouraged a mood favorable to political change, and the voters returned the Blanco, or Nationalist, party to power. Traditional spokesmen for the church, the landed class, and the rural proletariat, as well as the principal entrepreneurial interests, the Blancos quickly disillusioned many voters, and in 1967 the Colorado candidate, General Oscar Gestido, was elected to the presidency. When he died of a heart attack shortly after assuming office, he was succeeded by Jorge Pacheco Areco, a young lawyer and professor generally considered a political lightweight.

Pacheco Areco's presidency was troubled from the very start. As the U.S. government publication previously cited explains, "When the Colorados returned to power in 1967, there was evidence of social unrest, especially in the ranks of organized labor and among pensioners whose real incomes were steadily declining and whose checks were often late in arriving."[30] It was in this climate that the Tupamaros made their appearance, first as a kind of collective Robin Hood, noted for robbing banks and casinos and distributing portions of the take among the poor.

In June 1968 Pacheco chose to impose a series of extraordinary security measures, which included price and wage controls and the prohibition of strikes and demonstrations; the most distasteful aspect of his rule, at least to civil libertarians, was his perpetuation of rule by decree and the freewheeling use of press censorship. The result was polarization of public opinion, in which the opposition Blancos lined up behind the president while his own party made common cause with the radical left. Above all, this publication continues, "the police and the armed forces, as a result of their role in enforcing the security measures and their increasing outspokenness on policies, had somewhat diminished their reputation for being apolitical."[31] (This last is surely a remarkable understatement.)

Now this is by all means a melancholy picture, and there is no point in defending the Pacheco government as a model of constitutional probity. Whatever casuistry the Uruguayan Supreme Court might employ to represent it as operating within the sphere of its legal powers, it is clear that in choosing to rule by decree and breaking the link of accountability, it divested itself of a good measure of its legitimacy. But whether this qualifies it for the rubric "fascist" is another matter.

Conclusion

Part of the problem here is an ambivalence on the part of Costa-Gavras (and a lot of other people, including me) in classifying governments that are politically and socially conservative and are willing to use extraconstitutional measures against their legitimate opponents. On one hand, Costa-Gavras seems to suggest (to judge by *State of Siege* and also *Z*) that in virtually *all* bourgeois governments it is the police who secretly rule and, when the civilian politicians try to control them, the police and military take power directly. ("Governments come and go; the police remain.") On the other hand, he intimates that the difference between bourgeois and fascist governments is really negligible, especially when viewed from the receiving end of a policeman's truncheon. This is an arresting thesis, to be sure, but it begs several crucial questions. Perhaps the Tupamaros were justified in using violence against a government that, though legally elected, had abandoned its commitment to constitutionalism. But since they were already engaged in their hit-and-run revolutionism before Pacheco's declaration of a state of siege, is it not possible that they are at least partly responsible for it?[32] What did the intensification of violence yield from the point of view of the Tupamaros? Did it lead to the release of political prisoners? Did it persuade Pacheco to lift the state of siege? Did it strengthen the hand of those within his government and party (they *did* exist) who argued that it was time to engage in a dialogue with the opposition? Of course it did none of these things. But for Solinas and Costa-Gavras the Mitrione affair was a highly positive event in the history of Uruguay. To be sure, they conceded, "Beginning in April, 1972, the National Liberation Movement suffered some reverses and the movement was badly hurt: underestimation on their part of the enemy's strength, a qualitative change in the repression, army and police applying an officially approved system of torture."

> But [Costa-Gavras continues] the Tupamaros opened a path which has gotten results on the politico-military terrain of armed struggle. They also had a decisive influence on the coming together of the various forces of the Left, which, for the first time in Uruguayan history, opposed a united front to the traditional party. In fact, there has been a profound change in the people's political consciousness.[33]

One wishes that Costa-Gavras had clearly specified what he considered the "results" obtained "on the politico-military terrain of armed struggle." Even as he spoke, the semimilitary regime of Juan Bordaberry discarded all pretensions to legality, closed *Marcha* (and nearly a dozen more publications), jailed the country's most distinguished novelist on a charge of "pornography,"[34] placed Uruguay in the Brazilian orbit, and seriously compromised its independence for the first time in more than a hundred years. Recent visitors to Montevideo (including me) find in it a troubling resemblance to the Vienna of *The Third Man*: a defeated city, a shell of its former self, whose total expiration is but a matter of time. In Bordaberry's Uruguay and now that of his successor, General Gregorio Álvarez—unlike that of Pacheco Areco—there are no investigative commissions of parliament (in fact, there is no parliament at all), no inquiring journalists, no Tupamaros; and, if things continue as they are now, there will be no Uruguayans.

According to a report published in the Argentine press, an increasing number of Uruguayans are expressing their "profoundly changed political consciousness" not by going over to the revolutionary left but by leaving the country altogether. Between 1968 and 1972 some 250,000 people emigrated—technicians, doctors, skilled workers, students, mostly between the ages of twenty and forty, many with small children. They are going wherever they can—many to Argentina, some to Brazil, others to Australia, Canada, or the United States. At the end of 1974 Uruguay had probably lost 400,000 people since 1968, about 15 percent of its total population and a far larger

29

percentage of its economically active population.[35] How those too old to leave will fare is not a pleasant subject for contemplation, but it is not to be supposed that they will provide the shock troops of a future "armed struggle."

To be sure, the Tupamaros alone cannot be blamed for what is really a vast national tragedy, but neither can they evade the partial responsibility that is theirs. In the final scene of *State of Siege* Santore's replacement arrives at the airport, and as his family is packed into the waiting car on the tarmac, one of the maintenance men gives him a piercing glance. We recognize him from before: he was there when Santore arrived; presumably he is a Tupamaro operative. The message is clear—the struggle continues. But only for the audience, which goes home after enjoying a thrilling evening at the cinema. For Costa-Gavras's Tupamaros live in a Uruguay that does not really exist.

Notes

1. Of course, there are scenarists who are attracted to Latin American themes primarily because they like to write about politics. For example, Franco Solinas, who in addition to writing film scripts is an active member of the Italian Communist party, has declared that "I write scenarios which generally deal with political themes because in my opinion politics is a fundamental matter. I'm not interested in psychological stories; I have no use for literature in the traditional sense, the continual repetition of the same old patterns turned out with varying degrees of taste and intelligence, and presenting problems that are always personal and in the end uninteresting. This sort of story can only serve to shock and confuse the audience and cannot give it a key for understanding reality." "Interview with Costa-Gavras and Solinas," in Constantin Costa-Gavras and Franco Solinas, *State of Siege* (New York: Ballantine Books, 1973), p. 141 (hereafter *State of Siege*).

2. This contradiction is apparently resolved for some by calling films such as *State of Siege* "fictional documentaries." (See Joan Mellen, "Film and Style: The Fictional Documentary," *Antioch Review*, vol. 32, no. 3 [1973], pp. 403–25.) Unfortunately this category could be meaningful only to professional film makers, critics, and political intellectuals—if even to them. The general public has but a slight grasp of the concept of cinematic fiction and normally regards even highly stylized political films as "real." When the film in question has all the rough edges of a television news film and rigorously replicates the setting and texture of an actual event, it is regarded as a documentary by the viewing public, and probably rightly so. Such concepts as "fictional documentary" strike me as casuistic devices intended to relieve the film maker of the full responsibility for the accuracy of his material.

3. *State of Siege*, p. 29.

4. Ibid., p. 44.

5. Ibid., p. 46.
6. Ibid., p. 47.
7. Ibid., p. 62.
8. Ibid., p. 73.
9. Ibid., p. 74.
10. Ibid., p. 100.
11. Ibid., p. 124.
12. Ibid., p. 154.

13. From *Dialogue before Death* (Washington, D.C., 1971); quoted in Nathan A. Haverstock and Richard C. Schroeder, eds., *Dateline Latin America: A Review of Trends and Events of 1970* (Washington, D.C.: Latin American Service, 1971), pp. 14–15. To judge by the rather curious syntax of the interrogator, these dialogues took place in English.

14. *State of Siege*, p. 139.

15. This was apparently the reason why the Allende government chose not to buy the film, after extending full facilities to the company when it was working in Chile (personal communication from a Santiago-based West German journalist).

16. This imagination excuses not even Claude Fly, the AID agronomist, represented as Mr. Snow in the film. As Costa-Gavras explains, Fly was an "intelligent, witty man," but "with all his sincerity" his report on the country's agriculture "could help bring about certain changes, but also—and above all—provide the United States with information on the country's agricultural situation." And what would the United States do with this information? Solinas suggests that Fly's report "would give a particular direction to the country's economy, indeed the direction most useful to the United States and the American economy. If Fly thought that a collective economy in agriculture would be more useful to the country's necessities, his plan would never be put into practice because it cannot be reconciled with the pattern and interests of the United States, or the interests of the bourgeoisie and national oligarchies allied to the United States" (*State of Siege*, p. 155). It is unclear whether Fly is a one-man barrier between latifundia and agrarian reform in Uruguay or whether his (presumably good) advice would be ignored by the government that dispatched him. It seems strange to those of us more familiar with the day-to-day operations of the U.S. government that at no point is it suggested that Fly's activities might lead nowhere—for good or for ill.

17. *State of Siege*, p. 41. The comment in brackets is not spoken in the film; whether it was excised for technical or for ideological reasons is not clear.

18. The total fixed investment in Uruguay declined from 17.2 percent of the gross national product in 1955 to 11 percent in 1964, "at which level the net capital formation would be virtually nil." "Uruguay: The Difficulties of Economic Reform," *Bank of London and South America Review*, vol. 2, no. 22 (1968), p. 559. U.S. investment in Uruguay actually dropped from $55 million in 1950 to $47 million ten years later. See Hugh Holly, "External Finance," in Claudio Véliz, ed., *Latin America and the Caribbean: A Handbook* (New York:

Praeger, 1968), p. 531.

19. Thomas E. Weil et al., *Area Handbook for Uruguay,* Department of the Army Pamphlet 550-597 (Washington, D.C., 1971), p. viii.

20. Two historical precedents come immediately to mind: Cuban dictators Gerardo Machado (1924–1933) and Fulgencio Batista (1952–1959). Where the local opposition poses no serious threat to the regime, the rule is obviously inoperative. Nor is it valid if the government in power is believed irreconcilably hostile to the interests of the U.S. investment community, as in the regimes of Ramón Grau San Martín in Cuba (1933), Jacobo Arbenz in Guatemala (1954), and Salvador Allende in Chile (1970–1973).

21. *State of Siege,* p. 80.

22. Ibid., p. 153.

23. Ibid., p. 146.

24. Ibid., p. 149.

25. Ibid., p. 151.

26. Ibid., p. 56.

27. See the discussion of Alec Mellor, *La torture: Son histoire, son abolition, sa réapparition au XXe siècle* (Torture: Its history, abolition, and reappearance in the twentieth century) (Paris: Presses Universitaires de France, 1949), pp. 193–247.

28. The recent report of Amnesty International on this somber subject should give Costa-Gavras, Solinas, and other Europeans who idealize the peoples (and indirectly the police) of third world countries some cause for reflection. In Latin America, this document points out, "police brutality and harsh prison conditions have long been a traditional and largely accepted part of the social structure." In such countries as Paraguay, for example, "the system of torture and repression is far less sophisticated than that of neighboring Brazil; yet it is extremely effective in a country like Paraguay with its history of dictatorship, low educational levels, and small town atmosphere." It takes due note of the assertion that Latin America is suffering from the "internationalization" of torture, ranging from "claims that Brazilian and U.S. personnel *are present* at torture sessions" in Bolivia, Paraguay, and Uruguay to allegations that there are special "torture schools" in Brazil attended by "security personnel from other Latin American countries, and claims that torture equipment is imported directly from other countries." It goes on to say, however, "owing to the very general nature of such allegations, and the lack of specific evidence, Amnesty International is unable to make any definitive comment upon them. It has, however, been frequently reported that the U.S.A. has financed and organized anti-subversive training courses for Latin American police units in Panama. It is also known that . . . the U.S. government has never publicly condemned the use of torture in Brazil and Uruguay. In financing and equipping the police and armies that have used torture, *it can be argued* that the U.S.A. bears a contributory responsibility for the methods used by those governments." In the case of Paraguay, for example, the U.S. government is taken to task for "never [having] officially acknowledged or taken steps to prevent the use of torture by a government which appears to

32

be very much within its sphere of influence." Amnesty International, *Report on Torture* (London, 1973), pp. 178, 179–80, 196 (emphasis added).

This is not the place to discuss the morality of U.S. foreign policy in a general sense, least of all during the age of Kissinger. We cannot fail to emphasize, however, the distinction between the participation of overachievers like Mitrione in the interrogation of political prisoners and the systematic export of torture devices and techniques. Further, although U.S. support for Latin American dictatorships may well be reprehensible, it is difficult to imagine how, once having seen the light, Washington could successfully persuade its Latin American friends to abandon their repressive and inhumane practices. For this and other difficulties inherent in the problem, see the searching discussion by William S. Toll, "Human Nature and Moral Choice," *Peace and Change*, vol. 3, no. 1 (1975), pp. 61–64. I am grateful to Professor Toll for making available a prepublication copy of his essay and also for calling my attention to the report of Amnesty International.

29. *State of Siege*, p. 153.

30. Weil, *Area Handbook for Uruguay*, p. 269.

31. Ibid.

32. As Thomas Perry Thornton points out, "While in some cases the refusal of the incumbents [in any political system] to make constitutional provision for the transfer of power compels the insurgents to resort to extranormal means, at least equally often the insurgents utilize terror because they lack the political strength to make use of constitutional procedures that may be objectively adequate and just. They attempt to provoke the incumbents into repressive measures, in order then to claim that the incumbents have made constitutional machinery unavailable." "Terror as a Weapon of Political Agitation," in Harry Eckstein, ed., *Internal War: Problems and Approaches* (New York: Free Press, 1964), p. 76. The Uruguayan case seems to fall somewhere between these two poles.

33. *State of Siege*, p. 147.

34. Claude Fell, "Uruguay: La grande offensive policière contre la liberté culturelle" (Uruguay: The massive police offensive against cultural freedom), *Le monde diplomatique* (Paris), June 1974, p. 14.

35. Julio César Villaverde, "De mantenerse el éxodo actual, Uruguay perderá a 15 de cada cien habitantes" (If present rates of outmigration continue, Uruguay will lose 15 percent of its population), *La Opinión* (Buenos Aires), March 30, 1974, p. 4.

3
El Salvador:
The U.S. White Paper
Reexamined

El Salvador is a Central American republic about which most U.S. citizens know next to nothing. Yet this tiny country, smaller than the state of Maryland, has become the eye of a storm over larger foreign policy issues. At the heart of this controversy is a white paper *(Communist Interference in El Salvador)*[1] released to support the administration's requests for military and economic aid to that country's beleaguered civil-military junta.

Background

The stated purpose of this brief was to present "definitive evidence of clandestine military support given by the Soviet Union, Cuba, and their Communist allies to Marxist-Leninist guerrillas now fighting to overthrow the established Government of El Salvador." Such evidence, it held, "underscores the central role played by Cuba and other Communist countries beginning in 1979 in the political unification, military direction, and arming of insurgent forces in El Salvador."

Specifically, the following propositions are advanced in the State Department's white paper:

• The Cuban government of Fidel Castro played a key role in 1979 and early 1980 "in bringing the diverse Salvadoran guerrilla factions into a united front."
• The Cubans provided "assistance and advice" to those guerrillas "in planning their military operations."
• A series of contacts between Salvadoran Communist leaders and key officials of several Communist states "resulted in commitments

Reprinted from *AEI Foreign Policy and Defense Review*, vol. 4, no. 2 (1982).

to supply the insurgents with nearly 800 tons of the most modern weapons and equipment."

- Two hundred tons of those arms were covertly delivered to El Salvador, mostly through Cuba and Nicaragua, in preparation for what turned out to be an unsuccessful "general offensive" in January 1981.
- A major Communist effort was made to "cover" bloc involvement in Salvadoran affairs "by providing mostly arms of Western manufacture."

In sum, the paper concluded,

> by providing arms, training, and direction to a local insurgency and by supporting it with a global propaganda campaign, the Communists have intensified and widened the conflict, greatly increasing the suffering of the Salvadoran people, and deceived much of the world about the true nature of the revolution.

The white paper was issued on February 23, 1981. Almost immediately it became the subject of heated controversy in Congress and in the press, and it continues to provoke considerable skepticism in liberal circles. Both Senators Claiborne Pell (Democrat, Rhode Island) and Robert Byrd (Democrat, West Virginia), for example, have wondered aloud at the documentary veracity of the paper. Columnist Jack Anderson has simply stated as if it were a fact that the paper was "later shown to have relied on highly questionable and probably forged documents." If this was the case, then the Reagan policy in El Salvador—and therefore, by extension, in Central America—would be based at best on self-deception, at worst on lies. Therefore an examination of this document and the points raised by its critics is a matter of something more than academic interest.

The White Paper

The white paper consists of two parts. One is an 8-page pamphlet that summarizes the evidence upon which the State Department based its conclusions. The other is a 170-page book of reproduced documents, together with their English translations and a chronology. These constitute what the paper's editors call "a very small portion" of two caches recovered in November 1980 from the Communist party of El Salvador (PCS) and in January 1981 from the People's Revolutionary Army (ERP). Somewhat gracelessly translated, they nonetheless offer a fascinating, perhaps unprecedented glimpse into the political universe of Central American revolutionaries.

The chief exhibits include notes on three meetings: one between representatives of the Salvadoran guerrilla leadership and Soviet and Eastern bloc representatives at the Hungarian embassy in Mexico City; another between the guerrillas and the Cuban Directorate of Special Operations; and another between a representative of the Nicaraguan Sandinista National Liberation Front (FSLN) directorate and the Salvadoran revolutionary Joint General Staff at a secluded location in Managua. The same staff departed from the Nicaraguan capital for Havana, where Cuban "specialists" added the final touches to the military plans for a "general offensive," which was, in fact, launched without success in January 1981.

The most important document provides details of a journey by Salvadoran Communist party chief Shafik Handal in June and July 1980 to the Soviet Union, Vietnam, the German Democratic Republic, Czechoslovakia, Bulgaria, Hungary, and Ethiopia. In Moscow he met with Latin American specialist Mikhail Kudachkin of the Central Committee of the Communist Party of the Soviet Union, who urged him to travel to Vietnam in search of arms. Kudachkin also offered to pay for Handal's trip. In Hanoi Handal met with high authorities of the party and state and there obtained a pledge of 60 tons of weapons as a "first contribution." He then journeyed to East Germany, where he was advised that nearly 2 tons of auxiliary equipment (not arms) had already been dispatched to Managua. The East Germans also pledged an additional DM 2–3 million worth of resources "not directly military" in accordance with "concrete requests from the Salvadoran side." They promised to provide training for military cadres "especially in covert operation[s]" and to continue to search for "solutions" to the problem of acquiring Western-made weapons for their Central American comrades.

In Czechoslovakia Handal was told that some Czech arms circulating on the Western market would be provided to the guerrillas. Their transshipment would be coordinated with the German Democratic Republic. The Bulgarians offered German-made weapons and other supplies. The Hungarians offered radios and other provisions and proposed to trade arms with Ethiopia or Angola to provision the Salvadoran guerrillas with Western-made weapons. In Ethiopia Handal received commitments for "several thousand weapons" and ammunition. Returning to Moscow, Handal was told "in principle" that the Soviets would agree to transport the Vietnamese weapons. Some weeks later several (unidentified) socialist countries doubled the amounts of assistance promised to the Salvadoran guerrillas.

What kinds of shipments actually took place as a result of these discussions? In late September 1981 the guerrilla logistics committee informed the Joint General Staff that 130 tons of arms and other military materiel from socialist countries had arrived in Nicaragua for transshipment to El Salvador. Because of U.S. pressure on Nicaragua, however, there was a one-month delay in moving the arms to El Salvador. Meanwhile, the Salvadorans received a $500,000 cash contribution from Iraq to facilitate their operations and to purchase supplies in both El Salvador and Honduras.

Then, in early November, the shipments from Nicaragua were resumed. At this point the warehouses in Esmeralda (Cuba) were said to be "filled to the brim with the shipments that arrived last week, over 150 tons," and an additional 300–400 tons were scheduled to arrive a few days later.

The concluding documents emphasize that the chief problem had become logistical. Because of careless planning, arms shipments were too closely bunched together to be absorbed in an orderly manner. New talks with the Nicaraguans on delivery arrangements were scheduled, and on this note the document sample ends.

Criticism of the White Paper

Criticism of the white paper has turned largely on the use of its supporting materials rather than on the authenticity of the documents themselves. In fact, through a somewhat disingenuous use of language, many opponents of the administration's El Salvador policy have implied, without actually saying it, that the documents are forgeries. One critic who has unequivocally affirmed that they are a complete fabrication is, curiously enough, a former Central Intelligence Agency (CIA) man, Ralph McGehee. His argument, however, is based not on the El Salvador materials themselves but on an extrapolation from other situations in which the agency, he claims, has engaged in the large-scale fabrication of Communist communiqués. He also assures us that "although Soviet or Cuban support to leftist movements in Latin America may occur, it has generally been impossible to document." This point, which does not in itself speak to the case in question, allows him to conclude that the materials published in the white paper "can *only* be the product of yet another CIA forgery operation."[2]

Rather more sophisticated objections have been offered by John Dinges in the *Los Angeles Times* and by James Petras in the *Nation*. Dinges sees a discrepancy between the figures in the summary pamphlet for arms shipments—800 tons promised and 200 tons delivered by the time of the planned offensive—and the quantities referred to in the documents themselves, which, he writes, "indicate that far lesser quantities were promised or in shipment, and only about 10 tons ever actually crossed the border." He also characterizes Handal's reception in Moscow as "cool" and cites one of the documents where fear is expressed that Soviet "indecisiveness" might jeopardize any promise of arms made by socialist countries. Dinges concedes, rather curiously, that "read literally," the documents in the white paper would support its conclusions. He adds, however, that "if the Soviet Union and Cuba were pulling the strings behind the guerrilla movement, as Secretary of State Alexander M. Haig, Jr., has charged, evidence of such control is not to be found in the captured documents."[3]

The "counter–white paper" by Petras takes a different approach. First, he broadens the scope of the debate by insisting that the State Department has purposely ignored "the political and social realities" of El Salvador "by excluding an account of the social forces involved in the opposition," which, he insists, are neither Marxist nor manipulated by Marxist forces. Second, he denies the criticality of Cuban sponsorship of revolutionary unity with the argument that "the unity of leftist forces was under way prior to December 19 [1979] as the result of increasing repression by the regime and pressure from the rank and file of all groups." Finally, echoing Dinges's point about the actual arrival of arms in El Salvador, Petras says that the "failure of the guerrilla offensive in January was in part the result of inadequate armaments coupled with massive infusions of U.S. arms to the regime's forces."[4]

The most spectacular break for critics of the white paper came on June 8 and 9, 1981, on publication of two stories—one by Jonathan Kwitny in the *Wall Street Journal* and the other by Robert Kaiser in the *Washington Post.*[5] For purposes of economy and because the two pieces are strikingly similar, only Kwitny's is dealt with here. In this piece, the State Department official who uncovered and assembled the documents in the white paper, Jon Glassman, is quoted as saying that parts of the paper are possibly "misleading" and "over-embellished."

> In a three-hour interview Glassman freely acknowledges that there were "mistakes" and "guessing" by the government's intelligence analysts who translated and explained the guerrilla documents. . . .
> But a close examination of the documents the State De-

partment has brought forward indicates that, if anything, Mr. Glassman may be understating the case in his concession that the white paper contains mistakes and guessing. . . .

A close reading . . . indicates, instead, that [the white paper's] authors were making a determined effort to create a "selling" document, no matter how slim the background material.

The story then presents in considerable detail what Kwitny regards as critical weaknesses of the white paper. These are, briefly, that several important papers were attributed to guerrilla leaders who did not write them; that the role of Castro in unifying revolutionary forces in El Salvador is not substantiated in the documents; and that these papers, if anything, suggest "footdragging in procuring and transporting arms" on the part of various countries, "particularly the Soviet Union." The *pièce de résistance* deals with the white paper's estimates of actual arms shipments.

"From the documents [Kwitny quotes the white paper] it is possible to reconstruct chronologically the key stages in the growth of Communist involvement." It [the paper] then lists as the fourth such stage "the covert delivery to El Salvador of nearly 200 tons of . . . arms, mostly through Cuba and Nicaragua." But nowhere in the documents is there any mention of 200 tons.

Mr. Glassman says "That [200 tons] comes from intelligence based on the air traffic, based on the truck traffic. In other words, it doesn't come from the documents. . . ."

Another frequently quoted statistic in the white paper is that "the series of contacts between Salvadoran Communist leaders and key officials of several Communist states . . . resulted in commitments to supply the insurgents nearly 800 tons of the most modern weapons and equipment."

The 800-ton figure also represents an extrapolation, Mr. Glassman says. He says he multiplied 130 (the tonnage of arms one document says are stored in Nicaragua) by six to arrive at "nearly 800."

Oddly enough, Document I, which provides the rationale for this extrapolation, seems largely given over to complaints by the unidentified author about the ineptitude of guerrilla leaders in even finding a meeting place and the *slowness* of arms deliveries from outside El Salvador.

The Criticism Examined

Leaving aside the single outright charge of forgery, critics of the white paper largely agree that its documents—in the words of James Petras—"refute the very case the State Department is attempting to demonstrate." Where this is not so, they are based on random calculations that in any case are not justified by the materials made public. Finally, the very failure of the guerrilla offensive in January 1981 merely underlines the insignificance or near nonexistence of outside aid. Let us examine some of these assumptions in greater detail.

Documents as a Source. Although the State Department made it known from the beginning that the document book released with the white paper constituted only a small portion of the two caches and that not all of its findings were based on these papers, critics continually look to the document book for what they have been flatly warned will not be found there.[6] The most egregious example deals with the 200 tons of arms actually delivered to El Salvador. It is quite true, as Kwitny (among others) writes, that "nowhere in the documents is there any mention of 200 tons." The reason—as Glassman told him—is that the figure comes from other intelligence analyses based on air and surface traffic.

In the *Wall Street Journal*, however, this statement is immediately followed by the assurance that the 200-ton figure was arrived at "by extrapolating the hauling potential of several trucks that were listed in Document N. . . . This document," Kwitny writes, "an undated, unsigned, and barely legible handscrawled sheet, lists four trucks, three of which are still to be bought or built, along with the numbers, totalling 21, under the headings 'sea,' 'air,' 'land.' "*As it happens, however, this is not how the intelligence community arrived at the 200-ton figure, nor was it an accurate account of what Kwitny was told by Glassman.[7] The reference to Document N is Kwitny's own.*

The disjunction between the white paper's findings and the document book is repeated later in a discussion of military aid promised the guerrillas by Palestine Liberation Organization (PLO) leader Yasir Arafat. By separating two sentences by nearly a dozen lines on another subject, Kwitny manages, first, to obscure the fact that this reference came from other intelligence sources and, then, when he finally reports the fact, to make it seem as if Glassman has been abruptly surprised by some inconsistency.

The three errors in the white paper that Glassman freely conceded—that the authorship of one document was possibly wrongly attributed to a particular individual, that Castro was wrongly cited as

40

talking about the unification of Salvadoran groups when he was in fact speaking about uniting Central American Communist organizations in support of the Salvadoran left, and that the summary pamphlet turned a third-person reference in the documents concerning Handal into the first person—are all irrelevant to the documents' authenticity and to their political significance. Nonetheless, *these* are the "mistakes, errors, and guessing" plucked from the Glassman interview by Kwitny and misleadingly turned into general characterizations of the white paper.

The Role of Cuba, the Soviet Union, and Other Socialist Countries. The white paper does not—as Dinges believes—accuse the Cubans and Soviets of "pulling the strings behind the guerrilla movement," but it does establish that both have played a crucial role in Salvadoran events. Without the Cubans and Soviets, there would still be serious political turmoil in El Salvador but on a completely different level, which would be far more amenable to an elected government. Document A, a letter from Handal to Castro dated December 16, 1979, thanks the Cuban dictator for "help" in "undertak[ing] a transcendental step"—namely, the signing of a unity agreement among various revolutionary groups. Handal promises to honor the agreement and remain "worthy" of Castro's example and of the "patient and wise work that Cuban solidarity has contributed" to bringing about that unity. The other documents leave no doubt that Cuba is the chief point of reception for Eastern bloc weapons in the Western Hemisphere, from which they are transshipped to El Salvador via Nicaragua. What is remarkable is that Castro has even admitted as much—some months after the failed offensive, to a visiting German Socialist leader. On that occasion he "insisted that the shipments had ended," although he did not specify when. He also added that "the Soviet Union had not been involved."[8]

If there is one point that the document book repeatedly substantiates, it is that the Soviet Union indeed did not wish to appear to be involved. That is why Handal was sent off to Vietnam, Ethiopia, and other Eastern bloc countries. The particular appeal of Vietnam is, obviously, its capacity to offer an abundance of captured American munitions. This much is shown by the inventories of arms uncovered in El Salvador and confirmed by subsequent rechecking of serial numbers against U.S. Army records.

It is true, as both Dinges and Kwitny point out, that in Document E, dated August 5, 1980, Handal is depicted as "concern[ed] as to the effects that the lack of decision by the Soviets may have, not only regarding the assistance that they themselves can offer, but also upon

41

the inclination of the other parties of the European socialist camp to cooperate." This fear, however, expressed at one particular point, proved groundless, as the other documents and intelligence reports confirm.[9] What the revolutionaries did not get is direct Soviet assistance. Without Soviet sponsorship, however, it is simply not conceivable that the countries of the European socialist camp would have cooperated. This is a point that is driven home in Document B, minutes of a meeting in the Hungarian embassy in Mexico City. There a member of the revolutionary coalition was reminded by the Hungarian delegate that "it is because of the [Salvadoran Communist] party that the socialist world opens the door to you. It was a different case in Nicaragua."

The Dimensions of External Arms Commitment. How did the State Department arrive at the conclusion that "key officials of several Communist states [made] commitments to supply the insurgents nearly 800 tons of the most modern weapons and equipment"? As we have seen, Glassman is quoted in the *Wall Street Journal* as saying that "the 800-ton figure also represents an extrapolation. . . . He says he multiplied 130 (the tonnage of arms one document says are stored in Nicaragua) by six to arrive at 'nearly 800.' " Glassman did not, however, simply pluck the multiplier six out of the air, nor are the 130 tons simply "stored" in Nicaragua. Document I refers to them as "one-sixth of all the material obtained that the DRU, the Unified Revolutionary Directorate [the coalition of Salvadoran guerrilla organizations], will have eventually concentrated in Lagos [Nicaragua]." The fact that this exhibit, as Kwitny writes, "seems largely given over to complaints about the ineptitude of guerrilla leaders in even finding a meeting place, and the *slowness* of arms deliveries from outside El Salvador" is simply irrelevant. What is at issue in this instance is the size of the external arms *commitment.*

Why did the January 1981 offensive fail? Was this due, as Petras claims, to "inadequate armaments coupled with massive infusions of U.S. arms to the regime's forces"? The result of any military engagement—particularly in revolutionary warfare—is always open to different assessments. In this particular case, however, the evidence we have points overwhelmingly in a direction opposite the one Petras would have us take.

First, Document P, dated October 29, 1980, complains that revolutionary propaganda has not been taking hold among the Salvadoran masses. "The popular sectors are becoming progressively confused and are being affected by the defeatist attitude [junta President José Napoleón] Duarte and his lackeys are trying to instill among the people." Although in "the interior of the country our military forces are engaged in heroic combat," the author says, "vast sectors of the population" are "unaware of this situation, which can be dangerously influenced by a defeatist attitude."

Second, the failure of the guerrilla offensive simply could not be due to "massive infusions of U.S. arms to the regime." The reason is astonishingly simple. Between 1977 and early 1981 no U.S. arms were sent to El Salvador. Plans to reequip that tiny country's armed forces were held up in the final weeks of the Carter administration while an investigation was launched to determine responsibility for the murder of four American nuns in December 1980. The arms embargo was lifted on January 17, 1981. *The guerrilla offensive was launched on January 10, a full week earlier.*

Conclusion

The controversy over the white paper—at least in mainstream forums and in the Congress—has really been something more than a debate over a government document. In a broad sense it reflects an unfortunate confusion between fact and policy, differences of opinion over the origins of revolution and over the importance of external aid to insurrectionary movements, varying perceptions of Soviet strategy, and—unavoidably—partisan interest. To the degree that such discussions help to sort out the options, risks, costs, and benefits, they are part of the foreign policy process in a democracy.

In the case of El Salvador, however, serious discussion must begin with the acknowledgment that there is no discrepancy between what the exhibits released in the white paper show and the position of the Reagan administration. For other reasons—which it remains the burden of others to provide—the Reagan policy in that country and, for that matter, in Central America as a whole may yet be shown to be ill advised. But that is a case that must be argued first by taking the evidence of outside involvement fully into account. Such evidence is now in the public domain, in the form of the white paper and its document book. Arguing around these or purposefully misrepresenting what they contain will not do. In that sense, the white paper constitutes a challenge that critics of the administration's policy have not even begun to meet.

Notes

1. U.S. Department of State, Bureau of Public Affairs, *Communist Interference in El Salvador*, Special Report No. 80, with accompanying documentary annex.

2. Ralph McGehee, "Foreign Policy by Forgery: The CIA and the White Paper on El Salvador," *Nation*, April 11, 1981 (emphasis added). In spite of the tone of certainty that pervades this article, the author does not claim CIA service in any Latin American country.

3. John Dinges, "White Paper or Blank Paper?" *Los Angeles Times*, March 17, 1981.

4. James Petras, "White Paper on the White Paper," *Nation*, March 28, 1981.

5. Jonathan Kwitny, "Apparent Errors Cloud U.S. 'White Paper' on Reds in El Salvador," *Wall Street Journal*, June 8, 1981; and Robert Kaiser, "White Paper on El Salvador Is Faulty," *Washington Post*, June 9, 1981.

6. What the white paper actually said was that its evidence, which consisted of "captured guerrilla documents and war materiel and *corroborated by intelligence reports*, underscores the central role played by Cuba and other Communist countries" in El Salvador [emphasis added]. Much of the information that the State Department possesses, it goes on to say, "has been acquired over the past year. Many key details, however, have fallen into place as the result of the guerrillas' own records."

7. "The thrust of the [Kwitny] article," Glassman publicly stated the day it appeared in the *Wall Street Journal*, "does not represent my views. Mr. Kwitny simply extracted from a three-hour interview, a few anecdotes to support a different point of view. The result is a story which does not accurately reflect my position." Department of State, "Daily Press Briefing," June 8, 1981, mimeographed, p. 29. In the specific case of Document N, I rely on Glassman's reply to a question submitted to him on January 15, 1982.

8. *New York Times*, April 25, 1981.

9. If the documents were a fabrication, one cannot help wondering why this sentence would have been allowed to slip in.

4

Nicaragua: Somoza, Sandino, and the United States

The emergence in Nicaragua of a regime hostile to the United States and allied to Cuba and the Soviet Union was bound to send many Americans to their history books. Yet two quite different purposes can and do motivate such exercises. One might, for example, hope to learn from past errors, with a view to preventing "other Nicaraguas" in the future. The scope of that effort, in truth, is a very large one, with ample room for honest differences of opinion over precisely where U.S. policies went off track—and what might have been done to get them back on. In this connection no one can doubt that a careful, dispassionate examination of U.S.-Nicaraguan relations over the past half-century and more is certainly in order.

The other "course of study," however, is quite different, both in spirit and in substance. Its effect, if not its intent, is to excuse the conduct of the present revolutionary regime in Nicaragua as a wholly justifiable reaction to past U.S. policies there. Some of what has been written under this rubric tries to pass itself off as history, when it is really nothing more than the manipulation of past events (or pseudo-events) in the service of some very current agendas. Fragments of this approach can be found in declarations by academic caucuses, in the editorials of the prestige and religious press, and even in pronouncements by members of Congress. In its purest form, however, this line of argument was stated by Richard Fagen in *Foreign Policy* magazine:

> In 1912 after three years of unsuccessful attempts by Washington to stabilize Nicaragua by political and diplomatic means . . . the U.S. Marines were landed. At stake were the outstanding loans of U.S. and European creditors, . . . also the possibility of canal-building rights through southern Nicaragua. . . .
>
> Only in 1933 did the occupying troops finally depart, leav-

ing in their stead the U.S.-created National Guard headed by General Anastasio Somoza García. For the next 46 years the Somoza family never relinquished direct control of the Guard, and seldom gave up the presidency. . . .

The senior Somoza ruled Nicaragua as a personal fiefdom, with the Guard as his private army and enforcer and with the continuing support and approval of the United States.

From the outset, the dynasty was welcomed in Washington as a solid pillar of pro-American and anti-Communist strength in an otherwise troubled area. . . . Until the early 1970s, through Republican and Democratic administrations alike, the Washington-Managua alliance seemed unshakable. . . .

So close was the identification of Washington's interests with the continued rule of the Somozas, however, that little actually changed . . . until the Carter administration took office.

On the other hand, the new administration also feared any alternative to Somoza that would not be firmly controlled by the most conservative of anti-Somoza forces. Meanwhile, Somoza's powerful friends in the U.S. Congress and elsewhere were doing everything in their power—in the name of anticommunism and hemispheric stability—to insure that the four-decades old policy of U.S. support for the dynasty continued.[1]

It is hard to imagine a more sweeping indictment, for it spares no president since William Howard Taft and very pointedly includes Jimmy Carter. Admittedly, this is the way many Nicaraguans—by no means all of them Sandinistas—have seen the history of their country. Insofar as the United States is concerned, however, it happens to be quite false. The facts are these: the United States intervention in 1912 was *not* principally inspired by the motives offered; Somoza did *not* rule with the "continuing support and approval of the United States"; the dynasty was *not* welcomed by Washington "from the outset . . . as a solid pillar of pro-American and anti-Communist strength," and the Carter administration did *not* insist on restricting the alternatives to Somoza to "the most conservative of anti-Somoza forces," unless, of course, one chooses to label anyone who is not a Marxist a conservative, and an extreme conservative at that.

What Fagen rather disingenuously withholds from his readers—and what many who repeat his argument in a watered-down form simply do not know—are the vastly complicated dynamics of Nicaraguan politics. We are thus prevented from reaching the conclusion that typically overwhelms those who bother to study the subject: that the problem in Nicaragua has not been U.S. power so much as a lack of it—an inability to shape developments there according to our own values and preferences. For when all due tribute has been paid to Nicaraguan nationalism and the right of self-determination, it is still true that had Washington been able to control its putative "alliance" with Managua fully, Nicaragua's political history would have been vastly happier—for the immense majority of its people, if not precisely for the particular political sect of which Fagen happens to approve.

In the present context, the history of U.S.-Nicaraguan relations is more than a matter of mere academic interest. The reason is quite simple. Many countries are capable of formulating and executing foreign policy without excessive reference to their national conscience. The United States, however, is not one of them. If we conclude that we have inflicted a great wrong on a small and defenseless people, we invariably ask ourselves, Who are *we* to criticize the way its present leaders put things right? or even say, We're just getting what we deserve. History thus used and abused leads to guilt, guilt to immobility. That is why on the subject of our present relations with Nicaragua some commentators continually refer to the past—or to what they imagine the past to have been. That is also why it is as much a matter of public policy as of moral housecleaning to set the record straight.

Pre-1912: Seeking Stability and Solvency

During the nineteenth century U.S. interest in Nicaragua was dominated by a peculiar fact of geography—the existence of a huge volcanic lake comprehending approximately a quarter of the country's breadth—that made Nicaragua a logical site for an isthmus canal. A short trench incised from the lake's western shore to the Pacific and a somewhat longer one in combination with the San Juan River to the Atlantic port of Greytown would have produced an interoceanic route, and at a cost presumably far lower than at any other point of the isthmus, since elsewhere the excavation would have to run the full width of the divide. Moreover, long before the capital and technology necessary to produce this miracle were readily available, a shipping and passenger service across Nicaragua was in operation through a combination of steamer and stagecoach under the patronage of Commodore Cornelius Vanderbilt.

Vanderbilt's experiment was of short duration—begun in 1851, destroyed in 1855 by a flooding of the San Juan River, and supplanted by the Panama Railway the following year. The idea of a Nicaragua canal nonetheless persisted into the early years of this century. A commission created by the U.S. Congress reported in 1897 that it was technically feasible, and President McKinley even recommended its construction in his annual message to Congress in 1898. For reasons extraneous to this narrative, the Congress decided in 1902 to build the canal in Panama instead. Construction began in 1904, and the canal opened ten years later. Thus in 1912, when marines first landed in Nicaragua, the question of an interoceanic route had already been settled—elsewhere.

With the new route fully operational in Panama,[2] U.S. policy in Nicaragua became virtually indistinguishable from that elsewhere in the region—to promote the basic stability and solvency of governments. Lacking both, these tiny nations (and therefore the approaches to the canal itself) might fall into the hands of some hostile power. Outright annexation was thought unlikely, but as Africa and China had recently demonstrated, there were other ways in which European powers could establish naval and strategic—not to say commercial—presences without the full encumbrances of formal colonialism.

In this connection, the internal political life of the Central American republics (and Haiti and the Dominican Republic in the Caribbean) offered ample grounds for concern. Perennial outbreaks of revolution endangered the lives and property of European residents, whose home navies were wont to demand pecuniary damages in an extremely forceful fashion. On one occasion German gunboats even threatened to destroy an entire complex of government buildings in the Haitian capital of Port-au-Prince if $30,000 were not collected within a matter of hours. Political instability also provoked serious interruptions in economic life, making it impossible for the states to service their foreign debts. Default was an open invitation for European creditors to seize customhouses and port facilities, as prologue—many Americans and Central Americans feared—to a more permanent political presence.

Thus at the heart of the region's international problems were an economic and a political backwardness each reinforcing the other. Ostensibly, public life was a contest between "Liberal" and "Conservative" parties; in reality, it was a conflict between contending clans, families, and their retainers—typically organized along regional or provincial lines. Because the resources at stake were so scarce, the struggle was one in which quarter was neither asked nor given. In truth, no ruling party could afford the luxury of losing an election, so that, conversely, its opponent was left with no other recourse than the crucible of civil war. "It too often resorted to savage reprisals when it came to power," diplomat-historian Dana C. Munro has written. "The cruelties practiced on political enemies engendered factional hatreds which were passed on from father to son and which helped to keep the revolutionary spirit alive."[3]

The State Department archives and also the published correspondence found in successive volumes of *Foreign Relations of the United States* for the years 1898 through at least 1914 unambiguously establish that in Central America and the Caribbean, U.S. statesmanship was obsessed with the search for policy instruments capable of breaking this vicious circle. All manner of devices were tried—"preventive intervention" under the Roosevelt Corollary to the Monroe Doctrine, customs receiverships, and debt refundings. After World War I the emphasis shifted to a nonrecognition of governments that had come to power by force and an attempt to replace private, party armies with a nonpartisan constabulary.

It goes without saying that none of these mechanisms were warmly appreciated by the governments concerned. Nor were they particularly effective—at least in the middle and longer term. But they were not inspired by uniquely sordid or selfish motives. The United States did not land troops or seize customhouses principally to protect its investors and bankers, for the rather undramatic reason that before 1914 U.S. economic involvement in the area (apart from Cuba) was insignificant and the major creditors remained to an overwhelming degree European. Doubtless such considerations existed in embryo, but they were unquestionably minor ones, Munro concludes, "compared with the desire to avert the danger that disorder would invite European intervention."[4]

The Era of Intervention: 1912–1933

Nicaragua was a particularly notable example of the failure of U.S. policy to achieve its announced goals—and for means and ends to stray rather further from each other than proportion and good sense should have tolerated. Nonetheless, U.S. military intervention there must be divided conceptually into two quite distinct periods. The first began in 1912, when marines were landed to stabilize a country torn by civil conflict (in the process, shoring up an incumbent Conservative government that was unpopular and probably unrepresentative even in the narrow terms of the day). It ended in 1927 with the Peace of Tipitapa, when the United States, in the person of Secretary of War Henry Stimson, negotiated a truce between Conservative and Liberal politico-military chieftains.

These years constitute opposite ends of a learning curve for U.S. policy makers and diplomats. At the beginning, they indeed relied on force alone. But by 1927 certain realities of Nicaraguan life managed to impose themselves, fostering a serious effort to address what today would be called the "structural" causes of instability. The first of these realities was that the Liberal party, supposedly less friendly to the United States than the Conservatives, could not be permanently denied access to power. Second, since no defeated party could ever accept the results of falsified elections, the marines would have to remain for several years to ensure the integrity of elections. Finally, since no victorious government could escape an armed challenge from its defeated rivals, private military and paramilitary forces would have to be disarmed and disbanded. In their place the marines would train a nonpartisan constabulary to preserve public order once the U.S. expeditionary force had departed. In effect, the United States proposed to give Nicaragua the national army it had never possessed.

From 1927 to 1933 the United States tried to put these hard-earned lessons into practice. The process turned out to be so nettlesome that even if the depression had not eventually intervened to force a drastic reduction of overseas commitments, by 1933 Washington would in all likelihood have been ready to withdraw its troops from Nicaragua in any case. One very large problem was the refusal of dissident elements of the Liberal party to recognize the Peace of Tipitapa. Led by General Augusto C. Sandino, they retained their arms to pursue a guerrilla campaign against U.S. and Nicaraguan forces for six years. Although Sandino's movement was centered largely in the mountain fastness of Nueva Segovia, in the northwestern part of the country, at several points it managed to threaten key cities, including at one point the capital, Managua.

Today Sandino is a brooding presence in Nicaragua—mutely peering down from dozens of walls, with others speaking on his behalf. But his real identity remains enshrouded in myth and misunderstanding. The Coolidge administration repeatedly referred to him and his followers as "bandits," which was patently untrue. But neither was he the Marxist social revolutionary depicted by U.S. Secretary of State Frank Kellogg and many years later (in a curious coincidence of needs) by a Nicaraguan government bearing his name. In reality Sandino was an adventurer, a born leader of men, and a clever Nicaraguan politician much given to self-dramatization. But he was also what he often represented himself to be—a man of principle, forced to defend his country against what he regarded as a humiliation of its national sovereignty. From the very beginning he promised to lay down his arms the moment the last marine departed Nicaragua—and he kept his word. Even more significantly, Sandino refused to be used by forces extraneous to his cause. Thus, although for a time in the late 1920s he received rhetorical (and some small material) support from both the U.S. and the Mexican Communist parties, he steadfastly refused to follow Moscow's dictates and even denied that a social revolution was necessary in Nicaragua. This eventually led him to sever personal and political relations with Farabundo Martí, a Salvadoran Communist who for a time served as the Comintern's envoy to the Sandinista forces.

Although Sandino "won" only a few of his encounters with the marines, his constant hit-and-run tactics succeeded in making Washington's policy of pacification in Nicaragua very expensive—in blood and treasure, as well as in Latin American and even domestic U.S. opinion. This made all the more urgent the formation of a professional military force in Nicaragua to take over from the marines, but that was the other large problem. For neither party in Nicaragua was particularly anxious to have a constabulary above politics—were such a thing even possible. Eventually Washington compromised with this reality as well, accepting a bipartisan officer corps in the hope of forestalling what it feared and what eventually came to pass—a force led by politicians of the party in power.

The National Guard of Nicaragua was thus organized under the twin pressures of time and circumstance. At first the infant force was officered by American marines, but by 1931 and 1932 most of these had been replaced by Nicaraguans quickly trained at the new La Loma Military Academy. Since most of the enlisted men were drawn from Nicaragua's underclass, there was no "training up" into the commissioned ranks. Instead, officer candidates were drawn from civilian life, which made their indoctrination into nonpartisanship a rather quixotic exercise.

The frantic search for reliable professionals to officer the guard led the Americans to Anastasio Somoza. A Liberal general and politician, Somoza had studied at business school in the United States and, though of undistinguished social origins, had managed to marry into an aristocratic Nicaraguan family. During the 1920s he had served as consul in Costa Rica, deputy minister of foreign affairs, and finally minister of foreign affairs. During the last phase of the marine occupation he was named chief director–designate of the National Guard. "The last appointment was partly due to the patronage of the American minister in Nicaragua," Neill Macaulay writes in *The Sandino Affair*. "The Minister and his wife were impressed by Somoza's absolute mastery of the American language, and were captivated by his effervescent personality." And, he adds in an acid afternote, "Mrs. Hanna thought Tacho Somoza a smooth tango and rumba dancer."[5] Somoza was also, however, an experienced, disciplined public official who put in long hours, scrupulously kept appointments, and in general impressed the Americans with his industry and serious attention to detail. The decision to make him director of the National Guard was far from illogical.

Sandino, Sacasa, Somoza

When the last American marine departed in 1933, the deeper realities of Nicaraguan politics rapidly floated to the surface, sweeping away what positive legacies remained of U.S. involvement. Things had begun well enough: the elections of 1932 (like those of 1928), supervised by the marines, were the freest and fairest in the nation's history. And shortly after his inauguration on New Year's Day 1933, President Juan Sacasa received Sandino in Managua to work out the details of a peace accord. Sandino agreed to give moral support to Sacasa's administration, in exchange for which he was allowed to keep a small remnant of his private army and his followers were assured of preferential employment on future public works projects. Disbandment of Sandino's main force followed, and the rebel general himself returned home to Nueva Segovia.

Almost immediately it became clear that General Somoza and the National Guard constituted a new kind of threat to peace and order in Nicaragua. Relations between Somoza and Sandino—never good in the best of times—rapidly deteriorated as guard units harassed the guerrilla leader's former followers. And as early as November 1933, the American legation in Managua began to receive information that Somoza was planning a coup to oust President Sacasa. In February 1934 Sandino came to Managua to discuss his differences with the government and the guard; a few evenings later he was brutally murdered by Somoza minions shortly after leaving a dinner with Sacasa in the presidential compound. Two years later Somoza deposed Sacasa and seized the presidency for himself.

No one can dispute that these exact events could never have taken place in Nicaragua without U.S. intervention in 1912. But the record is clear also on this: there was no direct relationship between the United States and the murder of Sandino, the overthrow of Sacasa, or even the creation of the Somoza dictatorship. None of these events figured in U.S. plans or policies, nor—even more important— were these events greeted by the State Department with satisfaction or even tacit approval. What is true is that beginning with the murder of Sandino, Somoza (and later his sons and political heirs) habitually *represented* their actions as having prior U.S. assent. For different reasons, both opponents and supporters of the regime found it convenient to accept this explanation, and both tirelessly propagated it in various forms for four decades.

What many Nicaraguans failed to notice—and what Somoza quickly learned to exploit—was a decided shift in U.S. policy just about the time that these events were unfolding. Over a rather long period Washington gradually recognized that constitutional democracy of the Anglo-Saxon type was not exportable to Nicaragua or, for that matter, to Haiti, the Dominican Republic, or Mexico and, further, that attempts to impose constitutional democracy in tropical lands were both costly and counterproductive. Despotism and military rule seemed the inevitable fruits of the Caribbean environment and, U.S. officials reasoned, we had best stop attempting to contravene the experience of history. As Arthur Bliss Lane, U.S. minister to Nicaragua from 1934 to 1935, confided to a friend toward the end of his mission:

> The people who created the G. N. [National Guard] had no adequate understanding of the psychology of the people here. Otherwise they would not have bequeathed Nicaragua with an instrument to blast constitutional procedure off the map. Did it ever occur to the eminent statesmen who created the G. N. that personal ambition lurks in the human breast, even in Nicaragua? In my opinion, it is one of the sorriest examples on our part of our inability to understand that we should not meddle in other people's affairs.[6]

Of course, it was far easier to reach such conclusions in 1935, informed not only by the wisdom of hindsight but also by the shift in economic and naval power in the area, than in 1912. For after World War I the threat of European intervention in the Caribbean had virtually disappeared, and political instability—far from being, as it once had been, an "international" problem—could now be regarded simply as a local matter. Somoza was no improvement over what the United States had sought to replace, but by the time he seized power, Washington had virtually abandoned its attempts to reform the Nicaraguans. Having struggled so hard to get off the treadmill of intervention, the United States—beset by the manifold ills of the depression—was not about to get back on it.

Somoza also benefited indirectly from a broader change in U.S. policy toward revolutionary governments or, more precisely, governments that emerged from the extraconstitutional use of force. Before about 1930 Washington had attempted to discourage violent political change in the area by withholding recognition from de facto regimes. In 1907 and again in 1923 it had even sponsored treaties—to which all Central American governments were signatories—to that effect.

Over time it became apparent that the punitive use of diplomatic recognition put the United States in a serious bind. As historian William Kamman puts it, "Washington had to do more than just decide which government was in control, it had to determine the legitimacy of [that] government."[7] This meant, perforce, that if the only regimes worthy of recognition were those that issued from the ballot box, then to have diplomatic relations at all with many Central American republics, one would have to ensure that elections occurred in the first place. This led almost unswervingly to military intervention, with all the attendant unpleasantness. It also provoked much nationalist resentment throughout Latin America, where the United States was not acknowledged to have the right to determine the appropriate form of political change for its neighbors.

On this subject the Mexicans were particularly vehement, and in 1930 their foreign minister, Genaro Estrada, went so far as to call grants of recognition "an insulting practice." According to what became known as the Estrada Doctrine, only *states* could be recognized; when a new government came to power—by whatever means—its *bona fides* were not subject to the value judgments of others. Of course, the Mexicans had in mind their own revolution of 1910, which was very different from the upheavals in Nicaragua, since it went far beyond a periodic shift in the fortunes of contending elites. That upheaval had swept away an entire host of social and economic institutions and in the process inflicted serious damage—both physical and legal—on foreign property and investment, much of it belonging to American nationals. For nearly a decade Washington attempted to influence events there by withholding (or granting) recognition to the various governments that succeeded the dictator Porfirio Díaz. Extrapolating from their own rather uncommon experience, the Mexicans declared conditional use of recognition an offense to sovereignty and the right of weaker peoples to self-determination.

Other Latin American nations picked up this theme, and it quickly became part of a package of demands for nonintervention thrust at the United States during the Havana Pan American Conference in 1928—the first such meeting at which American delegates were forced to confront a serious and unified opposition. The events of that meeting plunged senior State Department officials into a mood of sober reappraisal, and during the next four or five years there was a gradual reconsideration of U.S. policy. Matters were helped along by the coming of the Great Depression, which suddenly made the United States more attentive to its image in Latin America, whose markets—some New Deal planners imagined—held the key to domestic economic recovery.

In any event, under both the Hoover and the Roosevelt administrations, there was a gradual turnaround, generally associated with the Good Neighbor Policy. The marines were withdrawn not only from Nicaragua but from Haiti as well, and at the Montevideo meeting of American states in 1933 and above all at the Buenos Aires conference in 1936, the United States definitively renounced intervention as an instrument in its relations with other American states.

Meanwhile, in 1934 the Central American nations quietly abandoned their commitments under the 1923 accords and subscribed to the Estrada Doctrine. Between the Montevideo and Buenos Aires conferences, the United States followed suit; under the circumstances, it had no other choice. But in some quarters of the State Department, serious doubts persisted to the very end. One official pointed out, for example, that even if nonrecognition had not succeeded in preventing revolutions, unconditional recognition would surely encourage them. It would also reinforce the temptation to back "any strong man who came along," with the attendant risk of identifying the United States too closely with a tyrant who would eventually fall. By 1935 or 1936 such apprehensions were overwhelmed by other considerations. The United States signed the Buenos Aires accords, tacitly accepted the Estrada Doctrine, won plaudits from "liberal" Latin American publicists and statesmen, and indirectly strengthened strong-man regimes, such as that emerging in Nicaragua.

Monopolizing Corruption

Somoza seized the presidency of Nicaragua in 1936 and remained in office through successive "elections" in 1939 and 1947. He had just accepted his party's nomination for yet another term when he fell victim to an assassin's bullet in 1956. His tenure, by far the longest in Nicaraguan history, was made possible in the first instance by the National Guard. Unlike the Liberal and Conservative armies it replaced, the guard was more or less professionally organized and equipped; and, because it retained a monopoly of arms, there was no force in the country capable of challenging it. In this sense alone, Somoza was Nicaragua's first "modern" president. What was striking and unique, however, was the way he adapted modern institutions—not just a professional constabulary but eventually a rationalized administration, a central bank, public works, and economic development generally—to suit his dynastic needs.

The Somoza regime could thus be described as a patrimonial police state, but it was also something else: a peculiar kind of social revolution. Before 1936 Nicaraguan politicians tended to be gentlemen of property and refinement, recruited from the landowners and professional class of the country's two major provincial cities, León (for the Liberals) and Granada (for the Conservatives). Their views on political and social issues were probably no larger or more responsible than Somoza's, but theirs was necessarily a more impersonal approach to the business of government. Then, too, precisely because Nicaragua had been so unstable before 1936, opportunities in public service or diplomacy had been passed around rather generously, if a bit sporadically. Now all the lines of political ascent ran directly through one man, his family, and his retainers. As the regime consolidated itself over generations, it absorbed an increasing share of the perquisites of power—bribes, kickbacks, and concessions. Corruption became less democratic—and therefore more hateful.

This was a change; so indeed was the kind of man with whom the dons of León and Granada had to deal. Crude and brutal, Somoza possessed a sort of raffish charm, which captivated some foreign admirers but represented for the more traditional political class in Nicaragua the triumph of *mala educación*. The people he brought into government with him—with rare exceptions—were of equally undistinguished antecedents or personal qualities. If the U.S. legation in Managua held a somewhat jaundiced view of the opposition during Somoza's early years of power, it was partly because memories of the old system were so fresh and partly because it was too easy to evaluate the claims of displaced aristocrats at their true value. These men were anxious not to restore democracy to Nicaragua but merely to get back on the take (which was what *they* meant by democracy). The United States never accepted Somoza's charges that his opponents were agents of Nazism (before and during World War II) or Communism (thereafter). But it was not about to land marines to return things to the status quo ante-1927.

The United States and Somoza: Ups and Downs

Over the twenty-year dictatorship of the elder Somoza, relations between the United States and Nicaragua were far less cordial—or even consistent—than the term "Washington-Managua alliance" suggests. During the years 1936 to 1939, for example, U.S. diplomats maintained a discreet distance from the regime and repeatedly turned down its most frequent request—for military assistance. What suddenly brought Washington around was World War II. Somoza himself was invited to Washington, and eventually Nicaragua received $1.3 million in equipment under lend-lease. (In exchange, the United States obtained temporary rights to a naval base in Corinto.) Once the conflict ended, however, the United States pointedly refused Somoza's plea for allotments on a more continuing basis. One Pentagon official pointedly voiced the War Department's determination not to "burden the country with armaments" and added gratuitously that "military missions from foreign countries" in such places as Nicaragua "should be avoided at all costs."[8] A further attempt by Somoza to purchase arms on a cash basis was blocked by the State Department. "Any arms which we might ship to him at this time," the relevant memorandum read, "could only be taken by him, the Nicaraguan public, and by the other Republics of Central America and of the hemisphere as a demonstration of complete support for his plans." This impression, it added, "would not only be erroneous, but extremely embarrassing."[9]

In 1947, when Somoza prepared to run for "reelection," Assistant Secretary of State Nelson Rockefeller called in his ambassador in Washington to impress upon him the Truman administration's acute displeasure and warned that such an eventuality "might create difficulties . . . which would seriously affect relations between the two countries."[10] To show that it meant business, the State Department once again blocked the sale of weapons to the regime and even managed to pressure Canada and Great Britain into joining the embargo.

This was a nimble procedure, but Somoza was nimbler still. He withdrew from the race in favor of a puppet candidate, Dr. Leopoldo Argüello, who was "elected" in the usual fashion. Somoza, of course, retained control of the guard. The opposition in Nicaragua tried to persuade the United States to refuse recognition to the new government, but Washington opted for a different course, partly because the new president had quietly assured the American ambassador that he intended to be his own man. Once in office Argüello did in fact make serious attempts to curb Somoza's power. The two men fell to quarreling over who was in charge—of the guard and the country. President Argüello eventually demanded Somoza's resignation and (in a fit of almost inconceivable daring) his departure from the country. Somoza's response was to overthrow his own putative puppet.

The United States, abruptly departing from its own recent adherence to the Estrada Doctrine, now withheld recognition. Even a crude attempt by Somoza to exploit anti-Communism (in a new "constitution" that also made it easier for the United States to establish military bases in Nicaragua) left the State Department unmoved. But Washington changed course some months later, when other nations in the area either had recognized or were preparing to recognize Somoza and when it became clear that any sanctions short of actual military intervention were bound to prove ineffective. (For instance, having refused to sell the dictator warplanes, the United States found it impossible to block his acquisition of B-24 bombers from Brazil.)

Then, once again, international events converged to bring about a thaw in the diplomatic chill between Somoza and the United States. In 1944 a revolution in Guatemala had brought to power a generation of young officers and intellectuals imbued with vaguely leftist ideals. By 1952, however, under President Jacobo Arbenz, the principal prop of the Guatemalan regime had become the Communist-led Labor Federation. There is still considerable controversy over the exact nature of the relationship between the Arbenz government and the Soviet bloc. At the time, however, it was perceived by Washington as the opening wedge for Soviet penetration of the Caribbean, and operatives of the Central Intelligence Agency, working with right-wing Guatemalan exiles, staged a coup that overturned Arbenz in 1954.

By cooperating with the CIA in the Guatemalan affair—at least to the extent of acting as a conduit of arms to exile forces—Somoza was able to neutralize some of the opposition to him in the State Department. But he still could not obtain approval of his plans to purchase heavy military equipment from the United States; he circumvented the continued American embargo by turning to Sweden for P-51 fighters. Further, when he began to menace Costa Rica with his new weapons, Washington promptly dispatched navy planes from the Canal Zone to convince Somoza that—whatever unpleasantness might have been necessary in Guatemala—it would not tolerate his aggressive conduct against a democratic neighbor.

The Next Somoza Generation

After Somoza's assassination in 1956, the regime moved into a qualitatively different phase. It was still undemocratic and dynastic but became more complex and even—at least to 1972—more popular. The fallen dictator's two sons, Luis and Anastasio, Jr. (who was called "Tachito"), were forced to share power. Luis was elected by the Nicaraguan Congress to fill out the unexpired portion of his father's term and "reelected" in 1957. Tachito, who had been sent to American military schools and West Point, assumed control of the National Guard.

Since the two Somozas had very different notions of how to discharge their legacy, they were continuously at odds until Luis's death in 1967 ended the rivalry and left Tachito in complete control. Unlike his brother, Luis Somoza was a man of some political imagination, who envisioned for Nicaragua a modified "Mexican" solution. The Somozas would retain, perhaps even increase, their power and wealth, but the formal leadership of the country would devolve into the hands of a succession of puppet presidents. In 1959 Luis even restored to the Nicaraguan constitution an earlier article prohibiting consecutive presidential terms and succession to the presidency of any relative of the incumbent. In 1963 he selected Dr. René Schick to be the first of a new series of chief executives.

Luis also believed in governing with a somewhat less heavy hand than his father (or, as time would show, his brother). Restrictions on the press and on opposition political activity were loosened; the role of the Nicaraguan military was played down and its budget actually reduced. Some new programs of economic development—financed, to be sure, with foreign loans and often subsidizing inefficient Somoza family industries—nonetheless created thousands of new jobs and therefore broadened the regime's base of support. These years also coincided with the rise of Castro in Cuba, the Bay of Pigs, and the missile crisis, so that in addition to some marginal political improvement within Nicaragua, the Kennedy administration had other, more pressing reasons for dealing with the Somozas. It was just about this time that the United States began a serious program of military assistance to Nicaragua.

Even before the end of Schick's term, however, it was clear that a more impersonal form of *somocismo* would not work. Schick attempted to rein in Tachito and the guard as long as he dared; thereafter, he lapsed into impotence and alcohol. In 1966 Tachito finally arranged his own election to the presidency, and few observers doubted that he meant to remain in office for life. It was precisely this determination to withdraw his brother's modest concessions to pluralism that aroused so much resentment in the opposition and even in the Liberal party, to which Somoza nominally belonged. At the same time, there was much resentment of the tendency to enlarge the family's financial holdings at the expense of the state and other, less-favored entrepreneurs.

During Tachito's first term, a boom in international commodity prices and the ready availability of foreign credit muted some of the opposition to his rule, even to his fraudulent "reelection" in 1971. The real breaking point came in 1972, as a result of an earthquake that devastated the city of Managua. During the first critical days of the calamity, guard discipline virtually disintegrated, and troops openly looted stores and warehouses. (Many of the stolen provisions later appeared on the guard-dominated black market.) Somoza himself pocketed millions of dollars' worth of emergency relief from abroad; preferential allotment of what remained went to guard families and government employees. The government's handling of this crisis created new centers of opposition in the church and the business community, and by 1974 or 1975 the regime had entered into a period of decline from which it was never to recover.

The Dynasty Declines

It was during this first half of Tachito's presidency that the United States seemed to support the regime most strongly, largely because of the obsequious conduct of Ambassador Turner Shelton, whose excessive identification with the dictator created a scandal in Nicaragua and ripples of opposition within the State Department and his own embassy. Of course, many Nicaraguans could not be blamed for thinking that Somoza now had a blank check from the United States to do anything he wished, since this was the inevitable impression that the ambassador gave and that Somoza himself rebroadcast far and wide. Moreover, they were not privy to the relevant diplomatic correspondence, which told another story.[11] But after Shelton's recall in 1975 and his replacement by James Theberge, Tachito began to note a decided shift in the political winds from Washington.

No doubt to the end of his days Somoza was mystified by the change, largely because his knowledge of this country was distant and dated. Although he was largely educated here, his English was never as good as he thought it was, and it did not improve with time. His picture of the United States was, in truth, as dated as his contacts were unrepresentative of the U.S. mainstream: a 1940s collage of conservative Roman Catholic prelates, military officers, right-wing businessmen from Texas and Florida, and a handful of congressmen—the most vocal and active of whom was Representative John Murphy, with whom Somoza had gone to private military school in New York and who is now in federal prison after his conviction in one of the Abscam cases.

Further, Somoza's own diplomats and advisers in the United States were unrealistic and ill informed. His ambassador in Washington, Guillermo Sevilla-Sacasa, had been in place since 1943 and—though dean of the Washington diplomatic corps—had never managed to learn English. As to the dictator himself, with few exceptions his visits to Washington were fleeting and incognito. Thus he was never able to appreciate the degree to which he benefited from Americans' benign neglect and sheer ignorance of his country, which also explain the success for some years of the tiny Somoza lobby in the House of Representatives.

After his fall Somoza tried to credit the shift in U.S. policy to sinister forces in Washington. In fact, President Ford's instructions to Ambassador Theberge to distance himself from the dictator reflected nothing more than a sober awareness that since the earthquake in 1972 a dramatic shift had occurred in Nicaraguan politics. Opposition to the regime was more widespread than ever before and growing, and it was largely unrelated to the then-tiny Frente Sandinista de Liberación Nacional (FSLN, or Sandinistas). Rather, it embraced virtually every respectable interest outside the Somoza machine, including businessmen like Adolfo Calero and clerics like the archbishop of Managua, Monsignor Miguel Obando y Bravo. What Somoza never grasped was the degree to which such people (whose English was sometimes better than his own and whose knowledge of American democracy was far more profound) were able to reach the State Department and Congress on their own.

From 1975 on, U.S. policy was clearly aimed at getting Somoza to restore some integrity to Nicaragua's political institutions, through dialogue with the opposition and free elections. When it became obvious that he intended to do neither, Washington, in conjunction with other countries of the region, began to press him to resign. This telescopes, of course, a long and very complicated process. Over three years' time Somoza played cat and mouse with the opposition and the United States, in turn encouraging and then dashing hopes of a peaceful and negotiated solution.

During these tense and difficult months, relations between the United States and the Nicaraguan opposition became rather frayed. The opposition wanted Somoza out as expeditiously as possible and at the beginning at least could not understand why the United States could not easily accomplish this, since in their view his regime was utterly dependent for its very existence upon Washington's good will. The State Department and the U.S. embassy in Managua were equally anxious to see Somoza depart, at least after 1978, but also wished to avoid a power vacuum in which the radical elements in the revolution (that is, the Sandinistas) could seize power. That is why, for example, all of Washington's draft proposals included retention of the National Guard in some form or other. At the beginning the opposition largely shared these apprehensions; but as time wore on, it decided that even jumping into a void was preferable to continued rule by Somoza.

The State Department and the White House meanwhile debated to what degree it was possible or even proper to intervene in Nicaraguan events. This led, in the words of a former Carter administration official, to "policy paralysis." In the end Washington's modest proposals were rejected by the opposition and voted down in the Council of the Organization of American States, which had become involved in the mediation process. While the opposition quarreled among itself and with Washington, the FSLN closed ranks and projected an image of coherence and unity of purpose. After the last mediation effort in early 1979, it was obvious that in the event of Somoza's departure, the Sandinistas were bound to play a role in Nicaragua's future far out of proportion to their actual numbers. Fidel Castro himself recognized as much and, after having maintained a somewhat platonic relationship with the FSLN over its lean years, began now massively to ship arms to them.

Ironically, this was precisely the prospect favored by Somoza himself. By refusing to negotiate effectively with the mainstream of the opposition, over time he pushed them into an alliance with the Sandinistas. This was done very deliberately, so as to confront the United States with only two choices—Somoza's continuance in office or a Marxist-dominated government in Nicaragua. To the very end, of course, Somoza was convinced that if the two alternatives were thus starkly posed, the United States would be forced to come down on his side. It apparently never occurred to him that Washington might choose to interpret its own national interests differently or, even less, that it would be unable to make a determination one way or another and thus lose what control of events it might have had. Thus Somoza's own belief in his carefully cultivated image as Washington's ally may have proved the most critical element in his fall.

Lessons from the Past

If the history of U.S. relations with Nicaragua over the period 1912 to 1979 establishes anything, it is that even when it tried, Washington was unable to make that country behave like a democracy—even in the limited Latin American sense of the term. Intervention could eliminate private armies but not the influence of the military in politics; it could ensure honest elections at the bayonet point of a marine—but not one moment beyond it. Moreover, even after renouncing its policy of intervention, the United States was held responsible for every untoward event that subsequently occurred in the history of Nicaragua, simply because at one point the United States had been present as an arbiter of events.

Both policies—intervention *and* nonintervention—were equally frustrating. Nonintervention won out because it was, quite simply, less expensive and—at the beginning—more popular, if not with the Nicaraguan opposition at least with other Latin American countries. In later years the United States periodically vented its pique with the Somozas by recurring to milder forms of intervention—to no great effect. For example, U.S. arms embargoes tended largely to enrich other suppliers, and even the Carter administration's vote against Nicaraguan loans at the Inter-American Development Bank—though undoubtedly a psychological shock of major proportions—was not sufficient to force the regime to mend its ways.

The Limits of Power. The Nicaraguan experience also demonstrates the way that vast asymmetries of power operate in international politics. Because the sheer physical and economic dimensions of U.S. power were so overwhelming to Nicaraguans, they simply could not accept the notion that Washington did not possess an equally unlimited capacity to arrange their political life—and this in the face of demonstrated failure. Rather, the outcome of every event in Nicaraguan political history was seen as part of a conscious policy in which the United States always got what it wanted. Understandably, but also unfortunately, Nicaraguans generally failed to recognize the role of inertia and drift in the foreign policy of great powers, still more the failure of political will—a failure that occurred more than once across the years but most devastatingly in the final hours of the Somoza regime.

For the Somozas, it was precisely in the interstices of U.S. policy that they found their vital breathing space. Nicaragua was, after all, a very small part of the international picture of the United States, and at best only a modest amount of foreign policy energy could normally be devoted to it. For the Somozas, of course, it was 100 percent of *their* energies, and they saw no reason to cooperate with Washington in any measure they viewed as detrimental to their own interests. When conflicts arose, they simply held their breath and waited for a change in the weather. In this they were uncommonly fortunate. World War II, the Guatemalan affair, the Cuban revolution—each appeared at a critical juncture in the relationship, and each forced the United States to bend in the Somozas' direction. U.S. motives were by no means dishonorable—Hitler, after all, was certainly a greater menace to humanity than the elder Somoza—but this could not prevent the impact of the larger policy from being felt negatively in Nicaragua.

Somoza's luck finally ran out when events in a tiny Asian country more than 10,000 miles from Nicaragua knocked the moral under-pinnings out from under U.S. foreign policy. By 1976 or 1977 a new current was abroad in Washington and in the councils of its foreign policy establishment, one that emphasized "the ethics of clean hands" almost to the exclusion of "the ethics of consequences." Gone was the ice-cold pragmatism from which the Somozas had so often benefited in the past. This did not mean that Washington finally sympathized with the Sandinistas but rather that it concluded that the threat of Marxism in Nicaragua was no longer sufficient to coun-terbalance the brutality, the corruption, and above all the sheer un-popularity of the Somoza regime. The Carter administration hoped to the very end that the FSLN would be swamped by moderates once the dictator was gone. They were, after all, more numerous and more broadly representative of the political forces in Nicaraguan society. It was a pious hope and sincerely held but poorly founded: Nicaragua was in the midst of a revolution, not a presidential primary. In the absence of the concrete application of its power, Washington's pur-poses remained ethereal and ultimately irrelevant.

The Limits of Hindsight. No doubt there are other lessons to be learned from the Nicaraguan experience, and other historians will have plenty of time to offer them. But one point must be foreclosed: history *does not* tell us—and *cannot* tell us—precisely *when* the United States should have shifted its policy gears in Nicaragua, apart from never having landed the marines in the first place. Intervention dur-ing the 1920s was resented, and understandably so, by Latin Ameri-can publicists and American liberals alike, but so was noninterven-tion—equally—once the Somozas were in place. Washington should have seen that after 1936 the Somoza regime was moving Nicaragua into a qualitatively different kind of political system, one pernicious even by local standards; but the process of consolidation was slow, and by the time it was fully evident, World War II was upon the United States and indeed the entire world.

The State Department did attempt to rein in Somoza in the 1940s, but by that time the dictatorship was fully fleshed out, complete with U.S. journalistic, financial, and political connections. In the 1950s and 1960s other priorities in the region moderated Washington's zeal for political change in Nicaragua—and, in one unfortunate ambassadorial case, made things much worse. Arguably, the biggest opportunity squandered by the United States was the assassination of the elder Somoza in 1956. Had Washington intervened at that point, the re-gime would have been unable to extend itself into the next genera-tion. This would have required much more than an arms embargo or even the imposition of an economic blockade, however, and there is no assurance that it would have worked. It also presupposes that it would have been possible to discard utterly our commitment to non-intervention, for a cause that—whatever one might think of the Somozas—was certainly not a pressing issue of U.S. security.

Ironically, time has proved that the hobgoblin to which Somoza so frequently pointed was real. Events *have* established that Marxism, if not Communism, was the final consequence of his fall. Perhaps it need not have been that way, and it will be left to earnest American liberals and sober American conservatives to retrace the path that should have and, more important, could have been taken. This is an exercise, however, in which sympathizers of the new Sandinista dictatorship need take no part; they got the outcome they prefer. The floor belongs, rather, to those who carry their past concern for the lack of freedom in Nicaragua firmly and consistently into the present—and, if need be, into the future as well.

Notes

1. Richard Fagen, "Dateline Nicaragua: The End of the Affair," *Foreign Policy*, no. 36 (Fall 1979), pp. 180–81.

2. It is true that under the Bryan-Chamorro Treaty (1916) Nicaragua ceded to the United States (among other things) an option on an interoceanic canal. Of course, it was never built, and Washington probably never intended to build it. The proviso was part of a package of concessions intended to persuade the U.S. Senate to approve a controversial emergency loan of $3 million to rescue the bankrupt Nicaraguan state from the importunities of its British creditors.

3. Dana C. Munro, *Intervention and Dollar Diplomacy in the Caribbean, 1900–1921* (Princeton, N.J.: Princeton University Press, 1964), p. 11. This work gives an authoritative overview of U.S. Caribbean and Central American policy between the Spanish-American War and World War I.

4. Ibid., p. 16.

5. Neill Macaulay, *The Sandino Affair* (Chicago: Quadrangle Books, 1967), p. 237.

6. Quoted in Richard Millett, *Guardians of the Dynasty: A History of the U.S.-Created National Guard and the Somoza Family* (Maryknoll, N.Y.: Orbis Books, 1977), p. 184. This book is the best treatment of the Somoza regime. The reader may not find Millett's conclusions at all congruent with his evidence, which is exhaustive and authoritative.

7. William Kamman, *A Search for Stability: U.S. Diplomacy toward Nicaragua, 1925–33* (Notre Dame, Ind.: University of Notre Dame Press, 1968), p. 232. This book gives full and careful treatment to U.S.-Nicaraguan relations for the period from 1912 through the rise of Somoza.

8. Millett, *Guardians of the Dynasty*, p. 202.

9. Ibid.

10. Ibid., p. 203.

11. One of Shelton's political officers, James Cheek, effectively used the "dissent channel" of the State Department to contradict his superior's laudatory reports of the regime. In time Cheek was honored with the American Foreign Service Association's Rivkin Award for his courage and integrity.

5
Chile: External Forces and the Overthrow of Allende

At the time of the fall of Chile's President Salvador Allende in September 1973, there was a widespread presumption throughout Latin America and much of Western Europe that the United States had been deeply, perhaps critically involved in the turn of events in Chile. This presumption fed not only on a general mood of anti-Americanism generated by the Vietnam War or even on the accusation of Allende's collaborators after the coup but on release to the world press in March 1972 of documents stolen from the files of the International Telephone and Telegraph Company (ITT), one of the largest American corporate investors in Chile.

The documents appeared to reveal, among other things, the existence of a plot hatched by ITT in late 1970 that, with the assistance of the U.S. Central Intelligence Agency (CIA), would "plunge the Chilean economy into chaos and thus bring about a military uprising that would keep Allende out of power." [1] As subsequent materials were published on successive days by syndicated columnist Jack Anderson, the Chilean Congress voted on March 28 to appoint a commission of thirteen members to investigate the matter; in Washington the Subcommittee on Multinational Corporations of the Senate Foreign Relations Committee launched an investigation of its own but delayed publication of its findings until after the 1972 U.S. presidential election. [2]

More information on the U.S. role came to light a year after the coup as the result of a congressional indiscretion. In the spring of 1974 CIA Director William E. Colby briefed the Intelligence Oversight Subcommittee of the House Armed Services Committee on Chilean operations. For some inexplicable reason, the stenographer did not observe the normal practice of stopping the transcription of testimony at points when security-sensitive matters were broached. Representative Michael Harrington of Massachusetts, a liberal Democrat with a strong interest in Chilean affairs, presumed upon his membership on the House Foreign Affairs Committee to read the classified testimony, although he was not permitted to take notes at the time. In a subsequent letter to his committee chairman, Representative Thomas B. Morgan of Pennsylvania, Harrington reported that Colby had revealed the expenditure of nearly $8 million by the Nixon administration for covert political operations in Chile during the Allende period; the purpose of these activities, the letter explained, was to "destabilize" the Popular Unity government.

The ink on this correspondence was hardly dry before copies had found their way to the editorial offices of the *New York Times* and the *Washington Post*, whose subsequent publication of it forced President Gerald R. Ford to acknowledge publicly in a televised news conference on September 16, 1974, that the sums in question had indeed been deployed in Chile. But President Ford categorically denied any U.S. role in the coup itself.

At about the same time, Seymour Hersh, chief investigative reporter for the *New York Times*, published a series of articles that purported to outline the way in which the covert action funds had been spent in Chile. The article of September 20, for example, informed readers—on the credit of unnamed "intelligence sources"—that

more than $7 million [was] authorized for clandestine CIA activities in Chile . . . in 1972 and 1973 to provide strike benefits and other means of support for anti-Allende strikers and workers. . . . Among those heavily subsidized, the sources said, were organizers of a nationwide truck strike that lasted 26 days in the fall of 1972. . . . Direct subsidies, the sources said, were also provided for a strike of middle class shopkeepers and a tax strike, among others, that disrupted the capital city of Santiago in the summer of 1973.[3]

On September 24 Hersh followed this story with another, attributing to "an administration source with first-hand knowledge" the information that shortly after arriving in Chile in mid-1971 to succeed Edward M. Korry as U.S. ambassador there, Nathaniel Davis received a message from Washington "saying, in effect, 'from now on you may aid the opposition by any means possible.' " Yet "another source" is quoted as saying simply that the ambassador "had been told to 'get a little rougher.' " Finally, still one more unidentified source confirmed "Ambassador Davis' direct involvement."[4]

Such charges, particularly in the light of what had already been revealed in the ITT documents before Allende's fall, could not be ignored, and a lengthy congressional investigation followed. The body constituted to look into U.S. activities in Chile during the

Allende period was formally designated the Senate Select Committee to Study Governmental Operations with Respect to Intelligence Operations, but it has become better known through the name of its chairman, Senator Frank Church of Idaho. The Church committee was eventually responsible for the publication of four important documents—the hearings on covert action in Chile (December 4-5, 1975); a committee print (that is, a staff report that summarized testimony and presented the committee findings); an interim report on U.S. involvement in the abortive military coup in Chile in 1970; and a final report that supplemented and corrected several aspects of the interim report.[5] Somewhat parallel to the activities of the Church committee was a massive—and from a scholarly point of view quite impressive—study of U.S.-Chilean relations during the Popular Unity period by the House Committee on Foreign Affairs, an investigation that actually began some months before the coup and continued for several weeks thereafter.[6] It is on these documents and no other that all that is said to be known for certain about the U.S. role in Chile must rest. Therefore, the findings of these committees, particularly the Church committee, must be examined with extreme care to see whether they are in fact congruent with the charges that have been made against the U.S. government by those sympathetic to the Allende regime or, at any rate, philosophically opposed to covert action on the part of U.S. intelligence agencies.

This need to compare charges with documentation is all the more pressing because high officials of the U.S. government and distinguished members of the American intellectual community have accepted in varying degrees the responsibility for Allende's failure. The most egregious case occurred on March 8, 1977, when Brady Tyson, newly named U.S. representative to the United Nations Commission on Human Rights in Geneva, declared to that body that "our delegation would be less than candid and untrue to ourselves if we did not express our profoundest regrets for the role some government officials, agencies, and private groups played in the subversion of the previous democratically elected Chilean government that was overthrown by the coup of September 11, 1973." Although his statement was immediately disavowed by President Jimmy Carter and Tyson himself was abruptly called home for "consultations," the delegate himself insisted that his statement was "in the spirit of the Carter government foreign policy as I understand it."[7] Three years later former Attorney General Ramsey Clark, attending a conference on alleged U.S. crimes against Iran in Tehran, cited the Chilean case as one other wrong for which the American people would yet have to atone.[8] And historian Barbara Tuchman probably summarized best the views of many in the literary and academic world when she wrote that "a vicious tyranny . . . has descended upon Chile, with the assistance of the United States. . . . For the United States to interfere in the domestic affairs of a neighboring state in an attempt to thwart their legitimate operation is intolerable."[9]

Although a certain edge of partisanship can be detected in these comments—was not "Chile," after all, one more indictment in the bill of particulars against the disgraced Richard Nixon?—it was actually left to a Republican to summarize most explosively the thesis of American guilt. In the midst of the Church committee hearings, Senator Richard Schweiker of Pennsylvania burst out in anger to former Ambassador Korry:

> I think your actions in Chile have proved the Communists right. The Communists argued that we capitalists will never give Communists a chance to get elected through democratic means, and Socialists can never succeed in our kind of government because we would never let them. I never believed it and I didn't believe it until we come up here and say in essence that we'll overthrow the government, even if the chief of staff [of the Chilean Army] gets killed in the process, even if we have to buy all the newspapers, we'll stop them coming to power. We have proved Castro and the Communists right by our inept and stupid blundering in Chile, and that's my opinion. I have no more questions. [General applause][10]

It is of greatest importance to both countries to examine critically the thesis of American responsibility for Allende's failure. For Chile it can determine the degree to which the policies of Popular Unity were or were not inherently self-destructive and therefore whether they were well or poorly conceived. For the United States the implications are even broader, for in the wake of Allende's fall and subsequent revelations by congressional committees, new restraints have been placed on the instruments of American foreign policy, and, what is perhaps of greater moment, the United States as a society seems to have lost the moral equipoise upon which its entire postwar foreign policy long rested. If this drift in American mood is well founded in fact, then obviously it is well advised. But it is vitally important to make sure that the lessons of history are precisely those that history actually teaches. The case of Chile offers a unique opportunity to find out.

American Interest in Chile

Let us begin by noting that the United States had been deeply involved in Chile long before Allende's election. The motivation for that involvement, though certainly not devoid of economic considerations, went considerably beyond them. Chile was—in the words of Ambassador Korry—

> the most stable, tested, freest democracy in South America, a democracy which was of a totally different profile than any other country in Latin America. . . . Democracy in Chile meant exactly what it meant in the United States. Even more: it meant an unfettered press. It meant a multipartied Congress. It meant an independent judiciary. It meant an apolitical army, an army that had never participated in politics.[11]

That the ambassador may have spoken more warmly of Chilean institutions than perhaps was fully warranted is irrelevant here, for it serves to depict quite accurately how Chile was perceived by American policy makers. Precisely because it *was* seen in this light—as a mature and open arena for the competition of ideas and systems—it was selected as a "showcase" for the Alliance for Progress under President Kennedy. One result of this was the receipt of nearly $2 billion of aid (loans and grants) during the administrations of Presidents Jorge Alessandri and Eduardo Frei. This made Chile the largest per capita beneficiary of alliance funds in the hemisphere. But in the context immediately following the Castro revolution in Cuba, it also burdened Chile with the obligation to prove the most advantageous hemispheric battlefield on which to meet the Cuban challenge to Western ideals.

This aspect of U.S. policy meshed with the darker side of Chilean politics. For if American officials could celebrate the openness and civility of the political process in Chile, they had ample reason to be troubled by its highly ideological environment and the active participation of two large, well-organized, and (particularly in the case of the Socialists) imaginatively led Marxist parties. The situation was in some ways analogous to that of Italy, and it was indeed Italy that provided the metaphor for U.S. covert action in Chile during the 1960s.[12] This much is clear from the memoirs of former CIA Director Colby, who had designed and executed such a program in Western Europe during the postwar decade. As defined by him, it included efforts to "strengthen the center democratic forces—parties, cooperatives, women's groups, etc.—against the leftist challenge."[13] In Chile

71

this meant subsidies to a wide range of non-Marxist political organizations, publications, and labor unions, a practice that eventually ballooned to such proportions that it was frequently quipped in Washington and in U.S. embassy circles in Santiago—only half in jest—that an entire generation of Chilean public men and women had come to depend upon the CIA for maintenance of living standards to which they had, perforce, become accustomed.

The largest effort in the area of covert action made by the United States before Allende's assumption of power in 1970 took place in connection with the elections of 1964. On that occasion some $4 million was appropriated by the U.S. government in support of the electoral campaign of Frei, slightly more than half the victorious candidate's war chest, disbursed apparently without Frei's personal knowledge.[14] According to Colby, "In the subsequent years [that is, 1964–1970] at least that much money was . . . spent by the CIA to help keep Frei and other democratic forces in power," largely through "direct propaganda and election activities."[15] Later agency evaluations found that Frei would probably have won the elections anyway, but the abundant subsidy covertly tendered to the Christian Democrats enabled them to secure a solid majority for their candidate rather than, as was more typical in Chile, a mere plurality.[16]

Two forms of covert activity contemplated during the Popular Unity period were clearly eschewed in 1964, however. On that occasion the CIA refused when asked to act as a conduit for contributions by American businessmen to anti-Allende electoral forces; the agency did, however, use one Chilean-based corporate executive to channel funds that were represented to be private, when in fact they were foreign and public.[17] Nor did the agency explore the possibilities of a military coup in the event of an Allende victory. In fact, in the weeks before the elections of 1964, both the CIA and the U.S. embassy strongly turned aside suggestions in this sense dangled before them by some apprehensive Chilean military men.[18]

Whatever one may think about the propriety of these actions, they were "covert" in name only. The source of funding was obvious not only by its very magnitude but by the techniques employed, which were wholly evocative of an American campaign. These included "polling, voter registration, and get-out-the-vote drives."[19] As Ambassador Korry later recalled, during the period in 1967 when he was being briefed in Washington before taking up his post in Chile, "I was told, not asked, by well-known reporters of our leading media outlets, by Congressmen, Senators, and their staffs, of the very large United States role in the election of 1964 in Chile; that is, the large effort mounted covertly." If it was a secret, he added, for some years it had been one of the most poorly kept in Chile.[20]

Covert foreign funding of Chilean electoral campaigns had become such a way of life that in the period just before the 1970 presidential contest Ambassador Korry was approached for contributions by representatives of several potential candidates, including Frei's foreign minister, Gabriel Valdés, Radomiro Tomic, Alessandri, and even Allende—whose campaign manager demanded a cool million dollars. All these proposals were sharply rejected.[21] After the nomination process was completed, it was assumed that the United States would have no choice but to follow the now-established practice of providing massive financial support either to Alessandri or to Tomic. Instead, something quite different occurred—a lengthy series of delays, an eventual decision to support no particular candidate, and, finally, the allocation of sums estimated at between $425,000 and $1 million to fund a "spoiling" campaign, which would merely emphasize the dangers of a Popular Unity victory.[22] In addition, the CIA in Chile produced what is called "black propaganda," that is, materials apparently originating in the constituent parties of the Allende coalition, with a view of sowing dissension among them. In this connection, CIA funds were channeled to an unidentified small political group—presumably the schismatic Democratic Radicals—with a view to reducing the number of Radical votes for Allende.[23]

Although U.S. government policy did not lean to the support of a single candidate, the American business community in Chile not unnaturally preferred Alessandri, and as early as April 1970 a board of officers of various multinationals led by Chase Manhattan Board Chairman David Rockefeller began a series of representations in this sense to the State Department. Initially they offered to raise a common fund of their own—$500,000—to be dispersed by the CIA. When informed of this proposal, Ambassador Korry sent Washington what he has described as "a blistering cable of opposition." In addition, the ambassador found himself "subjected to the most intense, incessant pressures from the CIA and its Chilean allies (including Chilean-based U.S. business concerns) to have the United States commit its covert support to their candidate. I refused."[24]

Having failed to exact a decisive commitment to Alessandri from the Nixon administration, the multinationals were nonetheless offered by way of consolation the assistance of the CIA in locating channels through which funds could be covertly passed to his campaign. In effect, however, ITT was the sole recipient of these services. The CIA and officials of ITT in Chile worked together closely in this sense, and eventually "at least $350,000 was passed by ITT to [the Alessandri] campaign." A roughly equal sum was passed through

Chilean channels by other American companies, but, according to the Church committee report, "the CIA learned of this funding but did not assist in it." [25]

Even if one accepts unhesitatingly the most inflated estimates of U.S. financial involvement in the 1970 elections, it is obvious that far less was spent on that occasion than in 1964. Nor do financial figures themselves fully account for electoral outcomes—in Chile or anywhere else. In any case, to evaluate their impact fully—in 1970, at least—one would have to know more about the countervailing efforts on Allende's behalf. On this, Henry Kissinger, then national security adviser to President Nixon, has simply stated that "throughout 1970 we received credible reports that substantial covert funds and assistance from Cuba and other Communist sources were being funnelled to Allende." [26] The Church committee report refers to "CIA estimates" that "the Cubans provided about $350,000 to Allende's campaign, with the Soviets adding an additional undetermined amount." [27] In addition, one is faced with an apparent paradox: in 1970 Allende gained a considerably smaller percentage of the popular vote than he had in 1964, when covert support for his opponent was nothing less than massive. Undoubtedly the U.S. decision not to support a particular candidate dispersed energies and resources that had been more effectively marshaled six years before; further, in the opinion of CIA Director Colby, the decision to focus on a "spoiling campaign," though "certainly a cheaper . . . tactic, also proved to be ineffective." [28] But all of this only suggests that the Nixon administration might inadvertently have contributed to Allende's victory; it does not tell us for certain what the result would have been had the U.S. government become more actively involved in the campaign, as the American business community wished it to do.

Precisely why a Republican administration would remain so impervious to corporate appeals on matters Chilean is a very arresting question. The Church committee report speculates that the Nixon administration's putative "mature relationship" with Latin America—a deemphasis on aid and social reform—possessed a covert action corollary that likewise dictated a less vigorous involvement in the political process. In addition, the report suggests that the activities of the United States in 1964 had become too obvious to be really effective a second time. [29] Former CIA official Cord Meyer offers another, simpler answer: "Nixon tried to avoid fueling a fratricidal rivalry between the two non-Communist parties by denying funds to both of them." [30]

A somewhat more elaborate and presumably more authoritative explanation has emerged in the memoirs of Henry Kissinger, who cites three factors: Nixon's and his own preoccupation with "so many other crises," domestic and foreign; an incorrect estimate of the most likely outcome of the Chilean elections ("I knew too little about Chile to challenge the experts"); and bureaucratic infighting between the CIA and the National Security Council (NSC) on one hand and the Latin American Bureau of the Department of State on the other. The latter, according to Kissinger, disliked Alessandri for being "too old, in reality because he was considered insufficiently progressive." [31] So much was this the case, he insists, that the bureau actually preferred the risk of an Allende presidency to outright support of Alessandri. In addition, Kissinger ruefully recounts, these people "chose at this moment [1969–1970] to attack the very concept of covert support for foreign democratic parties which had for so long been a central feature of our Chilean effort." The resources for any attempt to block Popular Unity's access to power, these people argued, "should hereafter be found entirely *within* Chile." What this meant, Kissinger concludes, was the demoralization "of the very forces we wanted to encourage. . . . In a close election the resultant subtle change in the psychological balance could be decisive." [32] (That Kissinger believes this does not, of course, mean it was necessarily so, but it does provide some understanding of the forces and motives at work within the U.S. foreign policy apparatus.)

In any event, the so-called 40 Committee of the NSC, the body charged with monitoring covert action overseas, met to consider the Chilean elections only four times—once in April 1969, when it deferred any decision; again in March and June 1970, when it authorized the sums for the "spoiling" campaign; and finally in August 1970, at which point it was decided that nothing further could be done. Given the need for presidential approval of all its decisions and the subsequent paperwork, Kissinger writes, it is unlikely that even the relatively small sums allocated reached Chile "before the second half of July. And then the Embassy was constrained by instructions that made their effective use almost impossible." [33]

These deliberations took place against the background of repeated polls that—until quite late in the day—reflected a substantial Alessandri lead. By the time Washington's perceptions of Alessandri's prospects began to match evolving Chilean realities, a massive covert effort "had been foreclosed without ever being discussed, first with the argument that a substantial program was unnecessary, and later because it was then too late." By early September Kissinger became convinced that he had been "maneuvered into a position incompatible with my convictions—and more important, those of Nixon." [34] Thus Chile went to the polls.

U.S. Attempts to Prevent Allende's Assumption of Power

Allende's tentative victory on September 4—actually, a plurality that waited upon what was in effect a congressional runoff—fell upon the Nixon administration with an impact all the more explosive for being unexpected. The president, in Kissinger's vivid recollection, was "beside himself," insisting on doing "something, *anything*, that would reverse the previous neglect." Now that it was nearly too late, "all agencies threw themselves into a frenzied reassessment." Since the Chilean Congress was scheduled to determine the new chief executive on October 24, "we were forced to improvise . . . with no real preparation. With time running out, our actions were inevitably frantic." [35]

On September 8 and 14, the 40 Committee met to shape a response to the prospect of an Allende presidency. That effort eventually ran parallel to—and at several points intersected—another that had been germinating for some months in the Washington, New York, and Santiago offices of ITT. For reasons of both chronology and clarity, the activities of ITT are discussed here first.

Activities of ITT and the CIA. The Chilean elections were discussed at some length at the spring 1970 meeting of ITT's board of directors. At that meeting there was a consensus that, as things then stood, Allende would win the popular election. In view of the company's large stake in Chile—which included a majority share in the national telephone company and ownership of two major hotels—this matter could not be viewed with equanimity. Hence board member John McCone, a former director of the CIA, was instructed to seek out the agency's chief, Richard Helms, to inquire what plans were under way to assist either Alessandri or Tomic. At their subsequent encounter, Helms informed McCone that the 40 Committee had already decided not to undertake a major covert effort; something would be done within the existing budget, he said—alluding, apparently, to the "spoiling" operation—but no additional funds were to be authorized for other covert purposes.

McCone then informed ITT chairman Harold Geneen of his conversation but, to blunt its edge of disappointment, arranged with Helms for a meeting in Washington on July 16, 1970, between Geneen and William V. Broe, chief of clandestine services at the Western Hemisphere Division of the CIA. It was at this meeting, according to Broe's later testimony, that Geneen offered to raise an election fund of "substantial size" for Alessandri, to be channeled through the CIA. Broe turned aside the offer, which, he said, was inappropriate in view of U.S. policy—that is, not to support any particular candidate in the election.[36] As noted, however, the CIA subsequently agreed to assist ITT in identifying channels whereby corporate funds could be covertly passed to Alessandri. A second conduit was opened for ITT to the National party through the good offices of the station in Santiago, and representatives of the company and the agency in Chile met often to coordinate their work in the months before the elections.[37]

In the period after September 4 and up to the congressional runoff on October 24, ITT continued to be extremely active in exploring ways to forestall an Allende presidency. The most apparent opening was to persuade the Chilean Congress to confirm Alessandri rather than Allende. The former had, after all, won nearly as many popular votes as the victor, and if he could enlist a significant portion of the Christian Democratic representation in Congress, he could obtain the presidency. As conceived by ITT operatives and emissaries of Alessandri and reported in a confidential cable from ITT's Santiago office on September 17, once confirmed by Congress, Alessandri would immediately resign. This would pave the way for new elections, in which President Frei would then be eligible to succeed himself.[38] Although this was legal in the very narrow sense, it flew in the face of a well-established custom in Chile that the legislature confirms as president whoever receives a plurality of the popular vote; to break that precedent—with its attendant risks to the nation's political and institutional fabric—would require some additional persuasion.

To this end, at the September 9 ITT board meeting in New York, Geneen told McCone that the company was prepared to put $1 million "in support of any plan that [would bring] about a coalition of the opposition," presumably a series of bribes to Christian Democratic congressmen. McCone then met with Kissinger and Helms to transmit the offer, but since Kissinger's office did not get in touch with him subsequently, he assumed that the tender had been rejected.[39] Meanwhile Jack Neal, director of international relations for ITT's Washington office, approached a member of Kissinger's staff and also the office of Charles A. Meyer, assistant secretary of state for inter-American relations. Although some reference was made in these conversations to a "sum in seven figures," their burden seems to have been less an offer of financial assistance than an appeal to the Nixon administration to remain neutral "in the event other attempts were made to 'save the situation' in Chile."[40]

In the final days of September there was a sudden shift in ITT tactics. A report from Santiago on the twenty-ninth cast considerable doubt on whether the "Alessandri gambit" would work, since "the prevailing sentiment among the PDC [that is, Christian Democratic

77

congressmen who had presumably been individually canvassed] is said to favor Allende." These men would change their minds only if Chile seemed about to suffer an "economic collapse."

> The pressure resulting from economic chaos could force a major segment of the Christian Democratic party to reconsider their stance. . . . It will become apparent, for instance, that there's no confidence among the business community in Allende's future policies and that the health of the nation is at stake. More important, massive unemployment and unrest might produce enough violence to force the military to move.[41]

The same day Broe met in New York with Edward J. Gerrity, senior vice-president of ITT, at the behest of his chief, Helms. It was apparent that some change of heart had occurred at the highest levels of the U.S. government, since it was now the CIA that was soliciting the help of the company. In New York Broe presented Gerrity with a plan following an identical logic but fleshing out in considerable detail what was already on its way in barest outline from the company's Chilean operatives. Specifically, he suggested that (1) American banks should not renew Chilean credits or should delay in doing so, (2) American companies should impose calculated delays on liquid advances, deliveries, and shipments of spare parts, (3) pressure should be applied to already foundering savings and loan institutions, and (4) all technical help should be withdrawn and no technical assistance promised in the future. Broe went so far as to suggest that companies in a position to do so should shut down their Chilean operations altogether. He then handed Gerrity a list of companies and suggested that ITT approach them in this sense.[42]

When he reported back to Geneen, Gerrity expressed serious doubts that the plan would work, an opinion later seconded by McCone.[43] In any case, there were no takers among other multinationals or major financial institutions. This was foreshadowed at the September 29 meeting, when Broe told Gerrity that "of all the companies involved [that is, companies with investments in Chile], *ours alone* had been responsible and understood the problem."[44] On October 9, after some soundings had apparently taken place, Charles Merriam, ITT's executive representative for international trade, was complaining in a memorandum to McCone that

> practically no progress has been made in trying to get American business to cooperate in some way to bring on economic chaos. General Motors and Ford, for example, say that they

78

have too much inventory on hand in Chile to take any chances, and they keep hoping that everything will work out all right. Also, the Bank of America has agreed to close its doors in Santiago but each day keeps postponing the inevitable. According to my source, we must continue to keep the pressure on business.[45]

American banks proved particularly unreceptive to these appeals. Their executives, subpoenaed by the Senate Subcommittee on Multinational Corporations or interviewed by its staff, categorically denied having been approached at this time by the CIA, ITT, or Chilean nationals. While strictly speaking this may not be true, the subcommittee itself could find "no evidence of [their] involvement . . . in a plan to block President Allende's election [either by the Congress] or in a concerted effort to weaken him by creating 'financial chaos.' "[46] Contrary to the Bank of America's promise to ITT, it did not "close its doors in Santiago."[47] Further, during this period Manufacturers' Hanover Trust actually *increased* slightly its lines of credit to Chile,[48] as did the First National City Bank of New York; what makes the latter case particularly interesting is that the borrowers were Chilean government agencies rather than private individuals or firms.[49] Thus, for all the cable time, telephone calls, meetings, and lunches and in spite of the undeniably dramatic flavor of the discussions, *in an operational sense no joint ITT-CIA plan to bribe the Congress or unleash a financial crisis ever existed.*[50]

Although it runs slightly ahead of the story, something should be appended here concerning ITT's activities after Allende's inauguration. In early 1971 Merriam invited Washington representatives of major U.S. corporate investors in Chile to form an ad hoc committee to coordinate their responses to the new government. The first meeting—one of several—took place in January, attended by personnel from Anaconda, Kennecott, Ralston Purina, Bank of America, Pfizer Chemical, and Grace.

The purpose of this committee, summarized in a minute prepared by Ronald Raddatz, the Bank of America representative, was to apply "pressure on the [U.S.] government, wherever possible, to make it clear that a Chilean takeover [of American properties] would not be tolerated without serious repercussions following."[51] This pressure, Merriam later testified, was expected to convince the U.S. government of the desirability of blocking loans to Chile by multilateral credit institutions such as the World Bank and the Inter-American Development Bank; this presumably would confront Allende with an early prospect of economic collapse and persuade him to become more disposed to negotiate with ITT on terms more favorable to the company than had been anticipated.[52]

Apparently the Anaconda Corporation shared the notion that this was the best way to proceed against the new Chilean government.[53] It quickly became clear, however, that other companies were moving to cut their losses, strike the best deal with Allende they could manage, or collect their insurance from the Overseas Private Investment Corporation. For example, Ralston Purina's Washington representative, William C. Foster, attended only the first meeting of the ad hoc committee; thereafter he was forbidden by his superiors to continue. The president of Ralston Purina gratuitously added his opposition to the "basic approach suggested," although Foster understood the purpose of the committee to be not the coordination of economic warfare but stiffening the resolve of the U.S. government,[54] which was seen by committee members as far too conciliatory toward expropriating Latin American governments.[55]

After attending two meetings of the committee, Kennecott's representative, Lyle Mercer, concluded that "there was no particular value to us for continued participation."[56] The Bank of America representative likewise withdrew after the second meeting.[57] Abandoned by three of the seven original members of the committee, ITT turned from its plans for economic disruption to the serious pursuit of a negotiated settlement with the Chilean government. These talks had actually begun at the same time as the actions just described, but apparently as a mere pro forma exercise while more adventurous strategies were explored. Having failed at the latter, the company was left with no choice but to behave responsibly and hope for the best.

Nixon, the CIA, and the Schneider Debacle: Tracks I and II. The sudden approach of the CIA to ITT on September 29 was a partial result of two meetings of the 40 Committee on September 8 and 14, 1970, whose purpose was to plot a response to the fact of Allende's electoral victory. These deliberations led to a decision to unleash a program of covert political activity to deny Allende the presidency through constitutional means (that is, some variant of the "Alessandri gambit"). The day after the second of these two conclaves, however, President Nixon summoned CIA Director Helms to his office and in the presence of Kissinger and Attorney General John Mitchell issued secret instructions to organize a military coup in Chile to forestall a Popular Unity government. So secret, indeed, were these orders that they were kept not only from the State Department and Ambassador Korry but even from the 40 Committee itself. To preserve cover, Helms was ordered to use a private reporting channel that would extend directly from the CIA station chief in Santiago to Kissinger or his military deputy, Colonel Alexander Haig.[58] The Church committee subsequently labeled these two different approaches "Track I" and "Track II" respectively.[59]

To implement Track I, on September 14 the 40 Committee authorized Ambassador Korry to enlist Frei's aid in rounding up congressional support for the "Alessandri gambit." To this end, a $250,000 contingency fund was set aside to bribe wavering Christian Democratic legislators.[60] When these efforts met with no success, an alternative version of the scenario was devised, calling for what would essentially be a "preventive" military coup. Under this plan—which Kissinger attributes to Korry and assumes was "cleared by associates" of the Chilean president—key ministers of the outgoing government would resign and induce their colleagues to follow suit. Frei would then have the option of replacing them with military officers. "In other words," Kissinger explains, "Frei was to be given the means to trigger a constitutional crisis—designed, as in every other scheme [within Track I], to lead to another election so that the country could choose between Frei and Allende, between democracy and potential dictatorship." Here, however, Washington encountered additional difficulties:

> There was doubt about Frei's willingness to do this [either]. The principal obstacle, however, was perceived to be the Commander-in-Chief of the Army, General [René] Schneider, who took the position that the politicians having put Chile into this mess, it behooved them to extricate her. Another stumbling block was reported to be the fear of the Chilean military that if they acted they would be treated like the Greek junta—that is to say, deprived of military aid by the United States and harassed by the left globally.[61]

The 40 Committee then ordered Korry to meet with military leaders and assure them that they had nothing to fear from the United States on this score but that, conversely, inactivity would lead to what they most wished to avoid—and on September 29 pipeline shipments of military equipment were held up precisely to make this threat credible. At the same time a propaganda campaign was mounted to convince Chileans, both civilian and military, of the economic ills that would befall the country in the event of a Marxist government. It was in this context, for example, that Ambassador Korry made his statement, much quoted subsequently, that in the event of an Allende accession the United States would not allow "a nut or a bolt" to reach Chile.[62]

81

On October 3–4, the Christian Democratic party assembled to consider, among other things, the attitude to be taken in the coming congressional balloting. On that occasion Frei made no attempt to persuade his correligionists to prevent Allende from assuming office. At the same time, it was clear to Washington that the military required additional pressure, and Korry was instructed to apply it.

What in effect was happening, as Kissinger has observed, was that Track I and Track II were merging, though without the knowledge of some of the principal American and Chilean actors. Korry thought he was still working for a "constitutional" coup, although without Frei's cooperation it is difficult to see how this scenario could be played out. Meanwhile, second-echelon elements of the same military who presumably would play a role in convoking new elections were being coaxed along a different path by the CIA. As the deadline date for the congressional runoff approached and the embassy's efforts proved increasingly fruitless, Nixon and Kissinger shifted emphasis—if not in intent, then by action and inaction—to an outright military coup.

The difficulties encountered along Track I paled into insignificance when compared with the obstacles faced by those who would implement Track II. Indeed, the latter could be mounted only over the loud and persistent objections of the intelligence community, who believed that conditions in Chile simply did not lend themselves to an adventure of this sort.[63] Nixon, whose respect for these people was not inordinately great in any case, waved their warnings aside; thus, between September 15 and October 20, the CIA made twenty-one contacts with key military and police officers in Chile who were known to favor such action.[64]

Recruiting "assets," particularly on such short notice, proved extremely daunting, for U.S. policy during the Frei years had systematically discouraged coup plotting among the military, as a result of which—in the words of one intelligence professional—the CIA had "deliberately distanced itself from those officers who were inclined to think in those terms."[65] Eventually the CIA narrowed its search to two groups—one led by General Roberto Viaux, who had been forcibly retired after leading an unsuccessful military revolt in 1969, the other by General Camilo Valenzuela, commander of the Santiago military district. Both had qualities that recommended them to agency operatives. Viaux, whose adventure the year before was ostensibly a protest against the budgetary neglect of armed forces personnel, was a popular figure among career enlisted men and junior officers and—since his retirement—a recognized figure in right-wing circles. As an active-duty officer in a key assignment, General Valenzuela was in contact with other senior military and naval figures and, what was more to the point, commander of the one garrison whose support was vital to success.[66]

Here again the obstacle was thought to be General Schneider. Failing to obtain his reassignment, the coup plotters decided to kidnap him and put him on a plane to Argentina. The CIA eventually decided in favor of the Valenzuela group; Kissinger says that Viaux and his associates were so informed on October 17;[67] the Church committee agrees.[68] The Valenzuela group carried out two abortive attempts—one on October 19 and one on the following day. One last effort was to be made on October 22. At 2 A.M. on the morning of that day, the CIA distributed to Valenzuela's men three submachine guns, some ammunition, tear gas grenades, and masks, all of which had entered Chile through the U.S. diplomatic pouch. Before this effort could actually be consummated, however, the Viaux group moved on its own. General Schneider's car was pushed off the road while he was being driven to work; the commander himself was shot and critically wounded when he reached for his pistol. The plotters fled, and the commander in chief died three days later in a Santiago military hospital.[69]

The Chilean military court that subsequently investigated the crime reported that General Schneider had been killed by handguns. These, in the findings of the Church committee, "were, in all probability, not those supplied by the CIA to the conspirators."[70] The committee also noted that an *unloaded* machine gun had been found at the site of the killing but professed itself "unable to determine whether [it] was one of the three supplied by the CIA."[71]

The U.S. Role November 1969–November 1970. If one assumes that the purpose of U.S. policy in Chile during the period under review was to prevent Allende's accession to power, one must confront the fact that virtually all American actions—whether by public or by private agencies—proved either irrelevant or counterproductive. The U.S. government's refusal to support a single candidate in the campaign obviously inflicted no harm whatever on Allende's quest and may even—if one accepts Kissinger's logic—have ensured his victory. Both the so-called spoiling campaign sponsored by the United States and the more or less independent funding activities of U.S. corporations on behalf of Alessandri seem to have had no decisive effect, at least in the direction desired.

In the period between election and inauguration, both ITT and the CIA, acting on instructions from President Nixon, explored various means of unleashing "economic chaos" in Chile, with a view either to convincing the Christian Democrats of the inadvisability of confirming Allende in the congressional balloting or to persuading the Chilean military in effect to nullify the elections so as to restage them later as a two-way race. At the same time, $250,000 was set aside to win the concurrence of Christian Democratic deputies and senators, and military shipments to Chile were held up to convince the armed forces that failure to act in a way desired by the United States would have very serious consequences.

So much for U.S. intentions; the results were quite different. The CIA and ITT found it impossible to enlist other corporations and the banks in the plan to unleash "economic chaos," and although there was a high degree of economic uncertainty during the weeks between Allende's election and his inauguration, it arose out of preoccupations quite logical in their own terms, not as the result of an orchestrated campaign or concrete economic actions, which the Senate Subcommittee on Multinational Corporations was utterly unable to document. Even in the areas under its direct competence, the U.S. government betrayed a remarkable lack of bureaucratic coordination; as I will demonstrate, even pipeline disbursements of nonmilitary aid to Chile continued unabated throughout this period.

Neither President Frei nor the Christian Democrats in Congress could be persuaded to play the role desired by Washington and the U.S. embassy in Santiago; consequently, the $250,000 that had been set aside *was never actually spent.*[72] The Chilean military could not be bribed negatively into sponsoring a coup, whether for new elections or some other purpose (Track I); when second-echelon figures in the armed forces were enlisted by the CIA to remove (not assassinate) General Schneider (Track II), a lack of control and discipline led to the precipitate events that climaxed in his death. The effect of the Schneider debacle was precisely the opposite of what was desired: it transformed the victim into a martyr to the "constitutionalist" traditions of the Chilean army; it encouraged other constitutionalist officers to support an orderly transfer of power to the new administration; and it discredited right-wing cabals both in the army and outside it.[73] Two days after Schneider's death, the Congress met and with impressive dispatch confirmed Allende as the victor in the presidential contest.

ITT fared no better in its efforts. Shortly after Allende's inauguration, the company found itself subjected to the same treatment accorded other large private economic concerns—the imposition of strict price controls combined with large mandated wage increases. In short order the company began to experience serious cash flow problems.[74] Eventually the Chilean state took over the Chilean Telephone

Company and offered to buy out ITT's local holdings for approximately $24 million. This was slightly more than one-eighth the company's own assessment of their book value, an appraisal that must have been closer to the truth since it had been paying premiums to the Overseas Private Investment Corporation for properties worth $108 million.[75] For some months negotiations between the company and the Chilean government dragged on with no visible result; the publication of the ITT documents by columnist Jack Anderson in March 1972 afforded the Allende regime a pretext to break off the talks. It was said—then and subsequently—that ITT deserved no better because of the role it had played in attempting to thwart Chile's democratic and constitutional processes. This argument would possess undeniable weight were it not for the fact that, by its own admission, the Chilean government had moved against the company's holdings in ignorance of the role that ITT had played in 1970 and early 1971.[76] Thus it cannot be doubted that even if ITT's conduct in Chile had conformed to the highest canons of corporate responsibility, it would have suffered precisely the same punitive and confiscatory treatment.

U.S.-Chilean Economic Relations during the Allende Government

That Allende's accession to power was not regarded as welcome news by the United States requires no further documentation. There was, in the first place, a significant economic interest in Chile that was endangered by the new government. This included approximately half a billion dollars' worth of investment exposure, a large part of which was insured by the Overseas Private Investment Corporation—that is, ultimately, by the U.S. taxpayer.[77] At stake also were some crucial ideological and geopolitical issues—issues that, in the retrospective view of both former President Nixon and former Chilean Foreign Minister Clodomiro Almeyda, far overshadowed economic questions.[78]

With Allende's election, a decade's worth of hopes, skills, and resources poured into Chile under the Alliance for Progress appeared for naught. A socialist state on the Latin American continental landmass posed the threat of a contagion that could not—as in Cuba—be easily confined within the boundaries of a single state. Chile might become a base for continental terrorist and extremist groups allied to the Soviet Union or Cuba. At a minimum, Allende's victory offered Castro a major opportunity to breach the wall of isolation that the United States and its allies had sought to erect around him.

In a global perspective, Allende's victory was also a serious setback for the United States. As Ambassador Korry subsequently remarked, at the very time when President Nixon was about to launch new diplomatic initiatives in Moscow and Peking, "to act indifferent to the disappearing . . . of a unique democracy in what was viewed throughout the world as [our own] backyard, could have a significant effect on those who made policy in the Soviet Union and the People's Republic of China." Further, with impending elections in Italy and France, "popular front tactics [could alter] the whole fundamental structure of Western defense, Western ideals." In this, he affirmed, "the Chilean model could have a certain effect." [79]

Whether such premonitions on the part of U.S. policy makers were fully justified is quite beside the point. These were the operative assumptions upon which the United States proceeded to deal with President Allende, notwithstanding some fulsome assurances by President Nixon that the United States was "prepared to have the kind of relationship with the [new] Chilean government that it is prepared to have with us." [80] Rather less clear, however, is the degree to which the United States was able to translate its concerns into an effective policy. Put simply, having established the fundamental hostility of the United States to the Allende experiment, we are still left to measure its effect.

Economic Relations and the "Invisible Blockade." The onset of serious economic difficulties after the regime's euphoric first year almost inevitably focused attention on relations with Chile's formerly preeminent partner in matters of trade and investment. The Popular Unity view of this matter was most definitively expressed by President Allende himself, in a speech to the United Nations General Assembly on December 4, 1972. On that occasion he declared that his country was the victim of "a new form of imperialism—more subtle, more artful, and for that reason all the more effective in impeding the exercise of our rights as a sovereign state." In this address Allende made particular reference to a "financial-economic blockade," "not an open aggression . . . but an attack at once oblique, subterranean, but no less lethal for Chile," whose purpose, he maintained, was "to isolate us internationally, strangle our economy, paralyze the sale of our principal export, copper. And to deprive us of access to sources of international financing." [81]

Since the 1973 coup, the concept of an "invisible" or "informal blockade" has been raised to the level of an omnibus explanation for the regime's most critical economic disjunctions. The subsequent publication by the Church committee of CIA Director Helms's notes taken during his September 15, 1970, meeting with President Nixon and Kissinger seems to provide confirmation of Allende's charges from U.S. official sources, since on that occasion Helms quoted Nixon as having ordered the CIA "to make the [Chilean] economy scream." [82] A corroborative piece of evidence—also uncovered by the Church committee—was National Security Council Memorandum 93 of November 1970, which established U.S. policies toward the new government. In the economic field, that document called for "all new bilateral foreign assistance . . . to be stopped. . . . The U.S. would use its predominant position in international financial institutions to dry up the flow of new multilateral credit or other financial assistance. To the extent possible, financial assistance or guarantees to U.S. private investment in Chile would be ended, and U.S. businesses would be made aware of the government's concern and its restrictive policies." [83] Here again, however, we must measure U.S. government *desires* against concrete effects.

Given the fact that U.S.-Chilean economic relations were dispersed along a rather broad front of activities, they must be explored layer by layer. Here I discuss the foreign debt, relations with the multilateral banks, relations with private banks, private suppliers of equipment and spare parts, and public (that is, government-to-government) aid programs. Finally, I review the credit available to Chile from alternative sources. Only then will it be possible to measure the approximate dimensions of the "invisible blockade."

The foreign debt. For some years before Allende's election, Chile had come to depend heavily on foreign borrowing to cover its trade and fiscal deficits. Such negative balances arose in part out of fluctuations in the world price of copper, whose volatile movements were capable of depriving the country almost overnight of resources needed to meet medium- and long-term commitments. Infusions of foreign capital—whether from governments, multilateral banks, or private foreign banks—eventually imposed an increasing burden of debt service, which as early as 1960 constituted 11 percent of the country's export earnings. Ten years later—that is, the year of Allende's election—that figure had ballooned to 37 percent.

Consequently, even before the advent of Popular Unity, international economists were beginning to worry about Chile; perhaps only the temporary boom in copper prices during the mid-1960s—producing the first trade surplus in many years—was capable of drowning out their warnings. Nonetheless, as one authoritative study recounts, "even in those prosperous days, [financial experts] were predicting that copper prices would soon fall and that Chile would need more than a billion dollars in new loans if the country was to continue to develop." In addition, it would require $600 million more for debt service. Because of the Vietnam War and the inflated price of copper, the exchange crisis predicted for the final years of Frei's administration was postponed for several years and in fact fell during the Allende period. It is worth noting, however, that even during the apparently halcyon Christian Democratic era, "Chile continued to experience a current account deficit during all but one of these years [1965–1970], and the country maintained its surplus only because foreign investment and external lending continued to be substantial."[84]

Without doubt the willingness of foreign creditors to extend new lines to Chile during this period constituted a vote of confidence as much political as economic; this was particularly true of those in the United States. But that confidence rested not merely on supposed ideological compatibility but on a vigorous Chilean program of improved tax collections, the projected expansion of copper production, and respectful treatment of foreign investment and foreign obligations generally. Further, these creditors were operating on assumptions about future events in Chile quite different from those that subsequently occurred. The political difficulties that erased the profit balances of copper mining under Allende simply were not anticipated, and even the relatively conservative projections that forecast trouble for the late 1960s assumed a far lower bill for imports and foodstuffs than materialized under a socialist government.

The long-avoided moment of truth came in November 1971, when President Allende announced a moratorium on foreign debt servicing and requested a general refinancing of Chile's international obligations. Between February and April 1972, Chilean delegates met for this purpose in Paris with representatives of the eleven nations holding shares in the country's public foreign debt.[85] In spite of the fact that some $1.23 billion of the total principal of $1.86 billion was owed to the United States, the United States was unable to persuade other members of the "Paris club" to link refinancing to compensation of the expropriated copper companies. Instead, the Chileans obtained a quite favorable settlement, which allowed them to roll over for an eight-year period 70 percent of the debts that matured between November 1971 and December 1972. In addition, a two-year period of grace was extended to the remaining 30 percent, which would otherwise have fallen due immediately. Finally, the Paris club members agreed to consider Chile's request for a rescheduling of the country's 1973 debt service at the end of 1972; preliminary talks on this subject finally opened after several postponements in May 1973 and were still in progress at the time of the coup.

88

Within the general framework of the Paris club agreements it was left to Chile to work out bilaterally the exact sums and interest rates with each of the creditor nations. As a result, the Allende regime obtained even more extensive relief. For no final agreement on the debts owed to the United States was ever reached, and the Allende government never actually serviced the amount that would otherwise have been remitted to Chile's principal creditor. This in itself constituted a de facto relief on foreign debt servicing for 1972 alone of approximately $243 million.[86]

The multilateral development banks. Chile fared somewhat differently at the hands of the Inter-American Development Bank (IDB) and the International Bank for Reconstruction and Development, more commonly known as the World Bank. Although both bodies had long supported Chilean efforts in economic and social development, during the Allende years there was a perceptible contraction in their financing role. Given the preponderant voice that the United States at least reputedly exercised in the deliberation of both bodies, many have concluded—along with President Allende—that political rather than strictly economic criteria determined the policies of both banks toward the Chilean government.

Sensitive to charges of this sort, both agencies have been at considerable pains to refute them. To this end, each issued a white paper documenting its dealings with the Allende regime. The IDB brief establishes the following points: (1) that two new "soft" loans were approved in early 1971 to expand the Catholic University in Santiago and the Universidad Austral in Valdivia; (2) that slightly more than $70 million—loans approved during the Frei administration—was disbursed to Chile during the Allende period, making the Popular Unity government the recipient of the largest annual disbursements in the bank's history; (3) that the bank received three new project requests during the Allende period, which were at various stages of study, none reaching the voting stage by September 1973; (4) that the bank rewrote an ordinary capital loan approved in 1969 at the Allende government's request in 1971 and by June 1973 had committed $13.1 million to this project—involving thirty-nine industrial ventures in which the Chilean State Development Corporation (CORFO) would own 49 percent of the stock—in addition to which it organized funding from nonbank sources bringing the figure to $54.2 million; and (5) that during these years the bank financed several million dollars' worth of capital imports to Chile from other member countries.[87] This still left, of course, no major *new* loans both approved and disbursed during the life of the Popular Unity government.

An independent study of Chile's relations with the multilateral development banks found the IDB guilty of a lack of consistency in lending policies, compared both with its past treatment of Chile and with its dealings with other Latin American nations during this period; but its critical focus centered on the failure to approve new loans (and what it regarded as an unreasonable delay in processing new applications) rather than on a lack of disbursements. It also suggested that IDB officials discouraged Chilean representatives from tendering certain kinds of loan applications in 1972 and 1973 on the grounds that, given Chile's lack of credit worthiness, such requests would not be favorably considered by the bank's executive board. Thus the fact that—apart from the two small university loans—no new projects actually came before the board for a vote during the Allende period could not, in this reasoning, have been due merely to technical problems or to Chilean restraint.[88]

What of the World Bank? Its own white paper recounted a close if increasingly troubled relationship with successive Chilean governments. On one hand, between 1948 and 1973 Chile received nearly $235 million worth of credit from this institution. On the other, in the half-decade before Allende's election, the bank began to worry about what it regarded as the country's deteriorating credit worthiness, its general economic performance, and its relatively high rate of inflation. So much was this the case that, apart from a large burst in 1967, presumably related to the copper expansion program, Chile received relatively little assistance from the World Bank during the Christian Democratic period, particularly when compared with the IDB or, for that matter, the U.S. government and U.S. private lenders (see table 5-1).

Against this background it is not surprising that the bank should voice serious reservations about Allende's economic policies—particularly his artificial acceleration of demand, cavalier treatment of inherited reserves of foreign exchange, and neglect of productive investment. Quite early (February 1971) bank officials warned Chilean representatives that the quest for wholesale "structural and institutional changes" added an element of "uncertainty" to the short-term economic outlook and reminded them that "the basic criteria of economic rationality and efficacy apply to socialist as well as capitalist-oriented economies."

During the first year of the Allende regime, the bank completed the preliminary studies for three new loans—one for electric power, one for livestock development, and one for fruit and vineyard processing. A conflict over electrical rates to be charged consumers

TABLE 5–1

LOANS APPROVED FOR CHILE BY MULTILATERAL BANKS, 1965–1973

(millions of U.S. dollars)

Fiscal Year	World Bank	Inter-American Development Bank
1965	4.4	4.9
1966	2.7	62.2
1967	60.0	31.0
1968	—	16.5
1969	11.6	31.9
1970	19.3	45.6
1971	—	12.0
1972	—	2.1
1973	—	5.2 [a]

NOTES: Does not reflect actual disbursements. Dashes indicate no loans approved.

a. Loan approved after September 11, 1973.

SOURCE: *Covert Action in Chile*, p. 34.

quickly caused the first to be shelved; the second and third were at various stages of completion when it became clear that the country could no longer service its foreign debt according to schedule.

During 1972 relations between Chile and the bank deteriorated, as the latter repeated its call for "an investment program setting priorities for the next several years together with an analysis of the monetary, fiscal, and balance of payments implications" that would allow a fuller evaluation of the country's credit worthiness. For their part, Chilean delegates at various meetings accused the bank of serving "not all its members, but [acting] as the mouthpiece or tool of special private interests of one of its member countries." On January 1, 1973, Chile suspended all payments of interest and principal on its obligations to the bank.

During the first six months of 1973 there were repeated attempts by both Chile and the bank to resolve their differences. By midyear the Chileans had agreed to resume service on their debt to the bank and to make good by December 31 the payments that were in arrears. In exchange, the bank authorized $5 million for feasibility studies that would justify future loans. At the time of the coup, however, no action on these had been taken beyond the preliminary paperwork.[89]

Unquestionably Chile's decision not to compensate the American copper companies damaged its credit standing in the United States, but whether this decision dictated bank policy is far from established. As World Bank President Robert McNamara reminded Chilean representatives in October 1972, the bank had a history of lending to countries that opted to nationalize basic resources—and this over the objections of one or more great powers. That difficulties between the bank and Chile occurred about (but not quite) simultaneously with the country's suspension of service on its public debt and that the Special Copper Tribunal refused to hear appeals by Anaconda and Kennecott at just about the time the bank was concluding (as the result of a special mission) that economic circumstances did not justify new lending to Chile do, however, provide some space for the dark inferences drawn by Popular Unity spokesmen at the time (and sympathetic commentators thereafter).[90]

Although Chile thus received no new loans from the World Bank during Allende's presidency, it fared only slightly better in the first two and final three years of his more moderate predecessor. This suggests a quite conservative lending policy generally—one that, on other grounds, might be the proper object of criticism. But with respect to the issue at hand, it strongly suggests—as the independent study cited above concludes—that the bank was "relatively consistent" in its treatment of Chile throughout both Christian Democratic and Popular Unity periods.[91] This rough parity of treatment is reflected in actual disbursements, which (on an annual average basis) were nearly the same under both regimes.[92]

Some confusion has been introduced into this controversy by the Church committee's publication of the contents of NSC Memorandum 93 and also by President Nixon's admission that after Allende's election he had instructed U.S. representatives at the multilateral banks to vote against Chilean loan applications.[93] But the truth is that—apart from the two university loans approved by the IDB in early 1971—no such petitions actually came before the executive of either during the Popular Unity years.[94] Was this the result of U.S. efforts? At the IDB there was considerable delay in processing applications, and it is known that bank officials actively discouraged new Chilean initiatives; when compared with its past role in Chile and its contemporaneous treatment of other member states, this points strongly to U.S. pressures within the organization. It is far more difficult to document such patterns at the World Bank. Without discarding the possibility that the United States *attempted* to influence the latter's dealings with Chile, however, it must be noted that whatever political pressures may have been operative in the first instance would inevitably have been overwhelmed in short order by economic criteria. That is, if one can look past the bank's historical lending policies, then up to the autumn of 1971 Paul Sigmund may be justified in remarking upon "a certain disingenuousness [on the part of the World Bank] in the constant reference to credit worthiness at a time when Chile was still paying her debts";[95] for 1972 and in 1973, however, Allende's own economic policies, undertaken independently and against the advice of World Bank technicians, were bringing about—ironically enough—precisely the situation that President Nixon would have willed if he could.

Relations with private U.S. banks. Private lending from the United States to Chile declined dramatically during the Popular Unity period. Cancellation of credit lines was gradual, however, and did not reach significant proportions until the fourth quarter of 1971—that is, after Allende's suspension of service on the public foreign debt.[96] The effect of this withdrawal of lending confidence was not negligible, since private U.S. banks had traditionally provided relatively low-cost money to finance imports and for rotating credits. There is no evidence of concerted activity, however, or even of financial "quarantine"; in mid-1973, for instance, the Bank of America was still involved in Chilean lending, both to local banks and to government corporations.[97]

Alexis Guardia, who served as an important economic adviser to President Allende, has since claimed that American banks withdrew credit lines pending resolution of Chile's external debt refinancing by the Paris club; however, he complains, "once an agreement was made . . . the U.S. banks did not modify their policy." [98] Guardia passes right over the fact that although the United States signed the Paris club agreements, those documents released Chile from its most pressing credit obligations while establishing that it would have to reach an individual understanding with each member country. The United States was never able to conclude a refinancing agreement with the Allende government. Nor can the conduct of U.S. banks be divorced from general business and economic conditions in Chile and the Popular Unity government's treatment of the banking sector.[99]

Equipment and spare parts. At the time of Allende's election most of the equipment in use in the most critical sectors of the economy— copper, steel, electricity, petroleum, and transport—was of U.S. origin. By late 1972, according to data cited from Chilean sources by the Church committee, "almost one-third of the diesel trucks at the Chuquiquimata copper mine, 30 percent of the privately-owned city buses, 21 percent of all taxis, and 33 percent of the state-owned buses in Chile could not operate because of the lack of spare parts or tires." [100] What was the nature of these shortages, and to what could they be attributed?

Court attachments of the assets of CORFO and the Chilean State Copper Corporation (CODELCO) in New York State in early 1972 made some Chilean acquisitions in the United States more difficult—more difficult but not at all impossible. First, these attachments did not affect private Chilean entrepreneurs, whose problems arose out of either a shortage of credit or their own government's foreign exchange constraints. Second, no restrictions were placed on the acquisition of parts for Chilean government entities by third parties—whether Chilean private citizens, Mexicans, or even Soviet intermediaries. Third, had the Chileans chosen to do so, they could have established purchasing agencies in other states. [101] Fourth, according to the testimony of two former functionaries of the Allende government, it was possible to acquire many spare parts from European and Latin American subsidiaries of U.S. companies. [102]

The problem of spare parts actually centered not on U.S. government restrictions, which did not exist, but on the availability of short-term credits. Indeed, in this connection it is not at all certain that the court attachments were really important, because by the time they were ordered in February and March 1972 the country's access to short-term financing had been seriously impaired by the moratorium on the foreign debt. Moreover, to the end of the Allende regime, it was possible for Chilean government representatives to purchase critical spare parts *for cash,* and in fact Norman Gall reported in mid-1972 that such parts were acquired for the Chuquiquimata mine and flown directly to Chile. One of the managers he interviewed at that mine even remarked in passing that "the freezing of our New York bank accounts . . . does not seem now to prevent us from buying supplies in the United States." [103] Likewise, at a meeting of major U.S. investors in Chile with Secretary of State Rogers on October 21, 1971, the representative of the Ford Motor Company reported that his company had "been asked to continue to supply spare parts to Chile." and that it had "indicated that they will, with firm letters of credit on reputable banks" (this in spite of the fact that its Chilean properties had just been expropriated and that the company had been forced to write off losses amounting to $16 million). [104]

It is true that at the same meeting Secretary Rogers "raised the question of whether there should be an informal embargo on spare parts and materials being shipped to Chile." But, according to the minutes, on this subject "the consensus of the group was quite mixed." Rogers urged the companies to hold periodic meetings with a view to "solidify[ing] a position." [105] No evidence has subsequently come to light suggesting that such an agreement was ever reached or implemented. Once again, by early 1972 Chile's credit standing imposed as serious a restraint on the acquisition of spare parts as any "informal embargo" might conceivably produce.[106]

Public aid programs from the United States. U.S. public aid to Chile—as expressed in loans and grants—fell dramatically during the Allende years, from an annual average (for fiscal years 1965–1970) of $119 million to slightly less than $7 million (1971–1973). To some degree the comparison is inevitably skewed by the fact that the Christian Democratic period was one in which Chile received unusually heavy assistance within the Alliance for Progress; further, the Nixon administration, whose views on aid to Latin America were (to say the very least) more astringent than its predecessors, began cutting back a full year before Allende's election. Thus the figure for total loans and grants authorized for FY 1970 (table 5-2) is significantly lower than for previous years, though still, of course, higher than the amounts appropriated during each of the three Popular Unity years.[107]

As the table demonstrates, U.S. public assistance during the Allende period was dominated by loans and grants for military acquisitions, which reached a historical high.[108] There was nothing particu-

---

TABLE 5-2

FOREIGN AID TO CHILE FROM U.S. GOVERNMENT SOURCES,
FISCAL YEARS 1967–1973
(millions of U.S. dollars)

	1967	1968	1969	1970	1971	1972	1973
AID [a]	15.5	57.9	35.4	18.0	1.5	1.0	0.8
Food for Peace	7.9	23.0	15.0	7.2	6.3	5.9	2.5
Export-Import Bank	234.6	14.2	28.7	3.3	0	1.6	3.1
Total U.S. economic assistance	258.0	95.1	79.1	28.5	7.8	8.5	6.4
Military aid	4.1	7.8	11.8	0.8	5.7	12.3	15.0
Total economic and military aid	262.1	102.9	90.9	29.3	13.5	20.8	21.4

NOTE: Corrections in addition made by author.
a. Agency for International Development.
SOURCE: *Covert Action in Chile,* p. 34.

larly sinister about this development, however. Allende and his ministers, Ambassador Davis has recalled, "requested and approved all credits, sales, training, and other [military] cooperation between Chile and the United States." The ambassador adds that "the consistent thrust of President Allende's public and private posture was to support military cooperation and credit and to criticize us if we showed signs of cutting back." What is perhaps of equal or greater moment, U.S. arms sales to Chile during this period were overshadowed by purchases from the United Kingdom and other Western sources.[109]

Important as it was, military aid was not the only form of U.S. assistance that continued under Allende. "Old" loans continued to be disbursed, amounting—according to one U.S. Treasury estimate—to "perhaps $200 million" for 1971 and 1972.[110] In addition, humanitarian aid—represented by the Peace Corps and the dispatch of surplus foods—was not withdrawn. It was shipment of the latter, including more than 10 million pounds of powdered milk in 1971, that "made it possible for President Allende to carry out his pledge to give a daily free pint of milk to every school child." [111] As table 5-2 indicates, in spite of President Nixon's decision to end all bilateral assistance not already committed at the time of Allende's election, new appropriations—however token in proportion—were nonetheless authorized during every year of the Popular Unity government.

The episode that placed U.S. assistance policies in the most unfavorable light concerned a Chilean attempt to borrow $21 million from the U.S. Export-Import Bank for the purchase of three Boeing passenger jets for the national airline (LAN). In August 1971—that is, one month after the expropriation of the copper mines but before a decision had been announced on compensation to the American firms—officials of the bank suddenly announced that they were postponing a decision on financing. The political motivations of this step seemed all the more transparent since it came some months *before* Chile declared a moratorium on foreign obligations. It seems probable that this move was taken at the behest of Treasury Secretary John Connally as part of a new hard-line policy toward expropriating third world countries in general and Latin America in particular.[112] From the U.S. point of view, however, the decision proved curiously self-defeating. The Chileans were not dissuaded thereby from deducting "excess profits" from the amounts due the American copper companies, and the Allende government—spurned in Washington—simply turned to negotiating with the Soviets for the purchase of Ilyushins.[113]

Alternative sources of aid. The withdrawal of lending confidence in

Chile by the U.S. government, the multilateral banks, and private U.S. banks was—from a purely quantitative point of view—more than amply replaced by credits from alternative sources. The precise amounts have escaped documentation, but in a very general way it is known that in the period 1970–1973 Chile's medium- and long-term debt increased by 16.7 percent while its short-term obligations grew nearly sixfold.[114] For 1972 alone, estimates of new lines of credit range from $600 million[115] to $950 million.[116]

The universe of Chile's new creditors embraced a remarkable range of political systems and ideologies. With Argentina, for example, a neighbor with whom relations had rarely been cordial and which at the time was ruled by a right-wing military junta, there was a significant growth not only in trade (largely foodstuffs) but in short-term credits, which, according to Almeyda, were critical in helping Chile to overcome balance-of-payments difficulties.[117] A somewhat similar relationship evolved with Brazil, whose military rulers were, if anything, even cooler to the Allende experiment;[118] for 1972 Brazil allocated $32 million to Chile, and the following year the Argentines authorized lines amounting to $100 million.[119]

With Western Europe economic relations were characterized— again, in the judgment of Almeyda—by "a friendly, cooperative, and favorable attitude";[120] if another former Popular Unity functionary is to be believed, by 1972 West European banks began to assume the role formerly played by their counterparts in the United States. By mid-1973, in his reckoning, "Chile had rebuilt and diversified its system of external finance." And, he adds, by June of that year the country had obtained from these sources short-term credits amounting to $547 million.[121] To which should be added the fact that Chile was able to draw from the International Monetary Fund for the period November 1970 to September 1973 an amount slightly greater than $100 million.[122]

Chile's economic relations with the socialist countries during the Allende period are still shrouded in controversy. According to the same Popular Unity source cited above, however, they were characterized by long-term grants of credit for the purchase of machinery and industrial plants, which reached $417 million by the end of 1972 (excluding grants from the Chinese). "In general," this commentator holds, "the monetary conditions attached to these credits were better than those of non-Socialist markets, at least as far as interest rates were concerned, for it varied between two and five percent, while no interest was charged for the Chinese grants, for which the first payment varied between 0 and 15 percent."[123] This seems a very generous interpretation of Soviet (and Chinese) accounting methods, but if it is true, in this particular area the refusal of U.S. credit sources to underwrite the Popular Unity government was for Allende an asset rather than a liability.[124]

The qualitative dimension that deprives these figures of much of their grandeur is the fact that for the most part Chile's new financial partners were unwilling to extend hard-currency loans. That is, most of the credits from sources both East and West were tied to specific projects or acquisitions; very little of them constituted "straight out balance of payments assistance—literally fully disposable convertible foreign exchange." Even the largest credit from the Eastern bloc—a $50 million loan from the Soviet Union authorized in late 1971—was believed by U.S. Treasury officials to be largely "project oriented and therefore susceptible to delays in disbursements." [125] "The overall picture," one sympathetic observer concludes, "is therefore that [Popular Unity] successfully obtained aid and credit to replace that withdrawn from the United States. The bulk of this credit," he adds, "was however short-term, involving harsher financial terms than in the past." [126]

"The invisible blockade": Toward an evaluation. The most obvious conclusion to all the material presented above is that there was no "financial-economic blockade" of Chile, invisible or otherwise. In sheer financial flows, the country continued to receive credit assistance from the widest variety of sources and in virtually unprecedented amounts. The refusal of the World Bank and the Inter-American Development Bank to countenance new loans (whether due to economic or to political motives) did not interrupt disbursements, which for the IDB reached record proportions. Even private U.S. banks and U.S. government agencies continued to transfer resources to Chile, though greatly reduced amounts. At no time was an embargo on spare parts or equipment imposed upon Chile by the U.S. government.

Even the legal judgments sought by Kennecott against copper shipments had only a tangential effect. At least, this is what a senior CODELCO official of the period tells us; after 1971, he writes, "the market for Chilean copper did not change in any substantial way." Although some supply routes had to be changed to circumvent orders of attachment in specific countries, "the fact is that Kennecott was unable to block the sale of El Teniente copper in Europe." [127]

To say that there was no blockade does not mean that Chile under Allende did not experience problems in its economic relations with the United States. Quite obviously the inability to reach a settlement on the portion of the public foreign debt owed to the United

States and probably also on the compensation due the copper companies had repercussions throughout the banking community and among U.S. creditors actual and potential. Above all, the reduction of short-term lines of credit immediately convertible into any currency introduced an "element of rigidity" into Chile's foreign trade transactions.[128]

That the U.S. government sought to use debt renegotiations to extract from Chile what it did not wish to grant—an end to deducting "excess profits" from the sums owed to Anaconda and Kennecott—does not mean, however, that in the absence of such demands its credit worthiness would have been instantly restored. "Refusal to grant aid to a nationalizing government is, after all, a perfectly rational decision," two British friends of Popular Unity have tartly observed, "since there is reasonable doubt whether the loans will be repaid." [129]

In examining the sorts of credits that Chile was able to obtain during the Allende years, two aspects command attention. First, they constitute attempts by newcomers or nontraditional creditors to take advantage of the U.S.-Chilean impasse, whether for economic or for political reasons, often at Chile's expense.[130] Second, the terms offered were generally so much less favorable than in the past that one cannot but think that the judgment of U.S. private bankers about actual Chilean credit worthiness was not far off the mark.

Finally, no evaluation of Chile's financial problems in this period can omit mention of the *advantages* that accrued to Chile by its failure to service its debts to the United States. This constituted de facto relief of $243 million for 1972 alone, which more than offset the loss of commercial credits from the United States,[131] although it could not fully cover the enormous balance-of-payments deficit. The dimensions of that deficit were indeed impressive but due entirely to elements beyond Washington's control: a drop in world copper prices, the increasing cost of foodstuffs, a decline in Chilean industrial productivity (particularly copper), and, above all, Popular Unity's own policies, which contemplated a painless transition to socialism in which the loyalty of some Chileans and the reluctance of others would be held in the one case and overcome in the other by an unremitting wave of consumption.[132]

Assistance to the Opposition, 1970–1973: The Dimensions of the Covert Effort

In its investigation the Church committee found that between 1971 and 1973 the CIA was authorized to spend $7 million "in covert support to opposition groups in Chile." Of this amount, $6 million was actually spent during the Allende presidency and some $84,000 thereafter for commitments made before the coup. If money spent during 1970 (that is, during the presidential campaign and before Allende's inauguration) is added, the figure rises to approximately $7 million, including project funds not requiring 40 Committee approval.[133] Obviously, it is these funds that lie at the heart of Representative Harrington's charge that the United States "destabilized" the Allende regime; therefore, the purposes to which they were put must be examined in careful detail.

Assistance to the Opposition Media. Ample evidence—both documentary and circumstantial—exists that significant portions of CIA money were passed to proprietors of opposition media during the Allende period. A Christian Democratic newspaper founded shortly after Allende's presidency, for example, closed for economic reasons within weeks after the coup. The television channel of the Catholic University and about two-thirds of the radio stations in Santiago were in the hands of opposition forces.[134] It is known for certain that *El Mercurio*, dean of Chilean dailies and the most sophisticated of conservative organs, received a covert subsidy from the United States of $1.5 million.[135]

The somber tones in which the Church committee presented these figures are considerably lightened, however, when placed in context. During the Allende period the media were subject to recurring waves of economic and political pressure. The Chilean government itself and state-owned industries together constituted the largest source of advertising in the daily press; the redirection of this business to exclusively progovernment papers, combined with the generally perilous state of private industry during this period, deprived the independent press of any visible means of support.[136] More to the point, efforts of the Allende government to bankrupt the only privately owned source of newsprint, the Compañía General de Papel y Cartones, failed only because of a National Freedom Fund subsequently believed to be underwritten by the CIA.

Newspapers and radio stations—along with other elements of the private sector—sustained losses produced by government-declared wage increases and price freezes. Bills for back taxes were presented under new interpretations of the law. Fire codes and other municipal violations were invoked against opposition newspapers and radio stations. When students of the University of Chile voted to change the orientation of their institution's television station, Popular Unity militants organized a takeover of the studios by the local union.

Import licenses and foreign exchange permits to acquire radio and television equipment and printing supplies were denied to unfriendly outlets.[137] In spite of all this it is true, as the Church committee somewhat artfully concluded, that "freedom of the press continued in Chile until the military coup of 1973";[138] this, however, was thanks not to Allende but to the CIA.[139]

Assistance to Opposition Political Parties and Movements. The greater portion of CIA money—approximately $4 million—went to the support of opposition political parties. This was used to underwrite the costs of their media, posters, campaign expenses, and salaries. The largest recipient was the Christian Democratic party, and smaller amounts were disbursed to the National party and various splinter groups. An effort was also made to split elements off from the Allende coalition, which may have played a role in the departure of the Radicals in late 1971. CIA funds subsidized the opposition in three by-elections in 1972 and in the congressional elections of 1973. The Senate investigators concluded on their own judgment that the agency had been crucial in forging "a united opposition." [140]

The Church committee found itself unable to say for certain whether the CIA had funded in any significant degree the activities of Patria y Libertad, a right-wing terrorist group that emerged early in 1971. This organization advocated violent resistance to the Allende regime, called for an insurrection within the armed forces, and took credit for fomenting the abortive military coup of June 29, 1973. "The CIA gave support in 1970 to one [unidentified] group whose tactics became violent over time," the Church committee's report somewhat tortuously reasons. "Through 1971 [Patria y Libertad] received small sums of American money through third parties for specific purposes," which activities it defines as demonstrations or propaganda activities, rather than violence. "Such disbursements—some $7,000 in total—ended," the committee concludes, "in 1971." Nonetheless, it adds, "It is possible that money was passed to [Patria y Libertad and other] groups on the extreme right from CIA-supported opposition political parties." [141] For his part, Ambassador Davis, who assumed his post in the final weeks of 1971, has simply stated that "to my knowledge, no monies or support of any kind were passed to Patria y Libertad during my incumbency." [142]

The support of non-Communist political forces in Chile was nothing new for the CIA; what were different were the circumstances. The Christian Democratic party, as Ambassador Korry later recounted, ended the 1970 presidential campaign owing "large amounts of money to banks the Allende government would quickly

101

nationalize; we reckoned that [the latter] would exploit nationalization to blackmail, to coerce, and to starve financially . . . numerous
and influential members of the party." This premonition, he adds,
was amply fulfilled "starting quickly in 1971." The vulnerability of
the Christian Democrats was apparent in that their party "owned no
national newspaper, had no TV outlet, and influenced few of Santiago's many radio stations at the time of the election"—a truly astonishing situation given the fact that it was the largest party in the country
and had been in government for six years.[143] In the context of an ever-
widening public sector under the control of Popular Unity, the prospects for the financial survival of the Christian Democrats, the Radicals, and other forces of the center were extremely problematic—or,
rather, would have been without external subventions.

Moreover, the Popular Unity government was not helpless in the
face of this challenge. "Most domestic and foreign newsmen in Chile
were aware," Ambassador Davis writes, "that government parties
skimmed a percentage off foreign trade operations." Further, "government transport, communications equipment, supplies of paper
and printing facilities were made available to the [Allende] forces on a
large scale. Subventions came from abroad. I believe most foreign
correspondents in Chile could confirm that the [government] parties
and candidates went into the elections of 1972-73 well supplied and
supported." [144]

In addition to funding political parties, the CIA provided financial assistance to a wide range of private sector groups, including
trade organizations and labor unions. It is here that the greatest controversy has arisen over the agency's role in Chile, since these groups
were responsible for organizing the two great national strikes (October 1972 and July–September 1973) that shook the regime, required
military participation in government, and arguably set the stage for
the coup. The Church committee has extensively documented the
degree to which the CIA made "a careful distinction between supporting the opposition parties and funding private sector groups trying to bring about a military coup." It confessed itself unsure, however—"given the turbulent conditions in Chile" and the close
relationship between various sectors of the opposition—whether such
a difference was operationally meaningful.[145] It goes on to say that

> with regard to the trucker's strike [July–September 1973] two
> facts are indisputed. First, the 40 Committee did not approve
> any funds to be given to the strikers. Second, all observers
> agree that the two lengthy strikes . . . could not have been
> maintained on the basis of union funds.

It remains unclear to what extent CIA funds passed to opposition parties may have been siphoned off to support strikes. It is clear that anti-government strikers were actively supported by several of the private sector groups which received CIA funds. There were extensive links between these private sector organizations and the groups which coordinated and implemented the strikes. In November, 1972 the CIA learned that one private sector group had passed $2,800 directly to the strikers contrary to the Agency's ground rules. The CIA rebuked the group but nonetheless passed it additional money the next month.[146]

The funds made available to these private sector groups were intended for relay to opposition political parties—in other words, to be tendered to such forces from the sources from which, under normal circumstances, they could expect to receive financial assistance. What was the "seepage factor" for nonelectoral purposes? Ambassador Davis has addressed himself to this question very fully:

> Obviously, if one gives a political party money to meet its needs, somebody or some group which otherwise might have contributed to those needs could not contribute to the truckers. But that is not the same thing as the party acting as a conduit. And it is not so difficult to tell if money given to a political party for electoral posters or advertisements, for example, is being used for that purpose.

To which he adds, with a droll touch: "The CIA has been paying monies in foreign countries ever since the Agency was formed, and has developed techniques of some effectiveness for determining whether its monies are being used for the purposes authorized and intended."[147]

This is not merely a matter of one man's opinion. Such information as has come to light on actual disbursements repeatedly points to a careful rein on such matters. In September 1972, for example, the 40 Committee authorized $24,000 in emergency support for one opposition group but deliberately withheld it from others for "fear that these organizations might be involved in anti-government strikes." The following month the committee allocated some $100,000 to private sector groups, which the CIA subsequently reported was spent exclusively on "election activity, such as voter-registration drives, and get-out-the-vote drives" in connection with the congressional elections of March 1973.[148] That this authorization took place in October 1972—a month characterized by widespread strikes against the Allende government—is far less suggestive than might appear at first glance, for such allocations required an additional six to eight weeks for disbursement. By that time, of course, the crisis in Chile had been temporarily resolved.

The most complete account of CIA deliberations on this subject and perhaps, given the chronology, the most important concerns August 1973. During that month the CIA station in Santiago recommended that an additional $1 million be granted to opposition parties and private sector groups. While the 40 Committee was considering the proposal, the station forwarded an additional plan to pass $25,000 to the striking truckers. The first proposal won approval, conditional, however, on the assent of the ambassador and the State Department. It remains unclear whether the second ever actually came before the 40 Committee. It is a matter of record that the initial proposal never received the necessary concurrence of the ambassador or the State Department and was therefore not implemented; the second, strenuously opposed by the U.S. mission, was never approved. *None of these funds ever changed hands.*[149] Meanwhile, events in Chile raced ahead of the deliberations in Washington, and the Allende government fell.

All of this still does not exclude the possibility that small amounts of CIA money found their way to the strikers. But official U.S. policy on the matter is unmistakable; and, assuming that the agency was faithfully pursuing the instructions it received (which the Church committee does not dispute), any major misallocation of funds by recipients would have been both obvious to it and the pretext for a policy review. Because the CIA believed that its money was being properly used,[150] no such occasion arose.

The United States and the Military Coup of September 1973. "Was the United States *directly* involved, covertly, in the 1973 coup in Chile?" To this rhetorical question, the Church committee report responds that its investigation "found no evidence that it was." It goes on immediately to qualify these findings, however, by observing that "the United States sought in 1970 to foment a military coup in Chile; after 1970, it adopted a policy, both overt and covert, of opposition to Allende; and it remained in intelligence contact with the Chilean military, including officers who were participating in coup plotting." [151] By this it is not clear precisely what the committee means us to understand. Either it wishes to convey the notion that, in spite of being unable to find any evidence, it refuses to abandon the presumption of guilt, or possibly it believes that between opposing Allende and fomenting a military coup there can be no meaningful distinction. Let us examine the evidential premises upon which the committee bases the statement just cited.

That the United States favored a coup in Chile during October–November 1970 is beyond discussion; it is likewise reasonable to assume that the desires of the Nixon administration became a matter of common knowledge among the Chilean high command as a result of probes made in connection with the Schneider affair. But once these efforts ended in disaster, how relevant were they to the subsequent U.S. role? On this the committee received two completely different views. One was the testimony of Thomas Karamassines, former CIA deputy director for plans and principal agency contact throughout Track II. In the excerpt published in the committee report, the following dialogue appeared:

> MR. KARAMASSINES. I am sure that the seeds that were laid in that effort in 1970 had their impact in 1973. I do not have any question about that in my mind either. . . .
>
> Q. Was Track II ever formally ended? Was there a specific order ending it?
>
> MR. KARAMASSINES. As far as I was concerned, Track II never really ended. What we were told to do in effect was, well, Allende is now President. So Track II, which sought to prevent him from becoming President, was technically out and done. But what we were told to do was to continue our efforts. Stay alert, and to do what we could to contribute to the eventual achievement of the objectives and purposes of Track II. That being the case, I don't think it is proper to say that Track II was ended.

When summoned before the committee, Kissinger took issue:

> THE CHAIRMAN. Would you take issue with that, with the [Karamassines] testimony?
>
> SECRETARY KISSINGER. Totally. *** It is clear that *** after October 15 that there was no separate channel by the CIA to the White House and that all actions with respect to Chile were taken within the 40 Committee framework. There was no 40 Committee that authorized an approach to or contact with military people, no plots which I am familiar with, and all covert operations in Chile after Allende's election by the Congress were directed towards maintaining the democratic opposition for the 1976 election. And that was the exclusive thrust, and if there was any further contact with military

plotting, it was totally unauthorized, and this is the first time I have heard of it.[152]

The subsequent investigation of the committee—far from resolving this controversy—only added to it by gathering evidence for a third version. This falls into three distinct chronological periods. Before October 1970 the CIA's contacts with the Chilean military were limited to two "assets," neither of whom—when President Nixon ordered implementation of Track II—was prepared to spark a coup. Under heavy pressure from the White House, the station rushed ahead to establish new contacts. After General Schneider's murder and the collapse of this initiative, the station was left "with only its initial assets in the military." It took the CIA another ten months to rebuild a network of agents "among the cautious Chilean military."

The second period began in the fall of 1971 and ran through the early months of 1972. By this time the Santiago station and CIA headquarters were discussing how to use the network of assets. The Church committee report continues:

In November [1971] the Station suggested that the ultimate objective of the military penetration program was a military coup. *Headquarters responded by rejecting that formulation of the objective, cautioning that the CIA did not have 40 Committee approval to become involved in a coup.* However, headquarters acknowledged the difficulty of drawing a fine line between monitoring coup plotting and becoming involved in it. It also realized that the U.S. government's desire to be in clandestine contact with military plotters, for whatever purpose, might well imply to them U.S. support for their future plans.[153]

In spite of these inferences, the report concludes that it was *this* period—some nine to twelve months before the Allende regime confronted its first serious crisis—in which the CIA was "most active" within the Chilean military. In this context, it refers to a "short-lived" effort to subsidize a small antigovernment news pamphlet aimed at the armed forces, the compilation of arrest lists and other operational data, and what it referred to as a "deception operation." The latter began as a plan to pass to senior Chilean officers counterfeit materials attempting to "prove" that Cuban secret police and the Investigations unit of the National Police (*carabineros*) were gathering intelligence prejudicial to the army high command. "It was hoped," the report explains, "that the effort would arouse the military against Allende's involvement with the Cubans, including the armed forces, to press the government to alter its orientation and to move against it if necessary." This proposal, it continues, was rejected by CIA headquarters, however, in favor of passing " 'verifiable' [true?] information to the leader of the coup group [*sic*] which headquarters and the Station perceived as having the highest probability of success." [154]

The third and final period embraced the second half of 1972 and all of 1973 up to the coup in September. Here the report concedes that CIA operations during these months were confined to intelligence gathering but once again manages to convey at the same time the unmistakable impression that such activities were virtually inseparable from coup plotting. It reports, for example, that during this period the Santiago station collected operational intelligence necessary in case of a coup, such as

> arrests lists, key civilian installations and personnel that needed protection, key government installations which needed to be taken over, and government contingency plans which would be used in case of a military uprising. *According to the CIA, the data was collected only against the contingency of future headquarters requests and was never passed to the Chilean military.* [155]

Then it reports that CIA "penetration" of various military groups known to be coup-prone

> was to walk a tightrope. The distinction between collecting information and exercising influence was inherently hard to maintain. Since the Chilean military perceived its actions to be contingent to some degree on the attitude of the United States Government, these possibilities for exercising influence scarcely would have to be consciously manipulated. [156]

As the careful reader will perceive, the second sentence in the paragraph above begins by presenting as a statement of fact what is nothing more than an opinion and concludes by declaring the United States guilty for purely contextual reasons. What is more important, the first sentence suggests an insensitivity on the part of the CIA to the possible consequences of intelligence gathering far greater than was in fact the case. During the secret testimony of David Atlee Phillips, former chief of the agency's Western Hemisphere Division, the elaborate precautions taken by CIA headquarters to avoid involvement in a coup in Chile were outlined in considerable detail. In its report, however, the Church committee chose not to take official cognizance of this evidence. It has only come to light in Phillips's subsequently published memoirs. There he explains that in May 1973 two cables were sent to the Santiago station.

In a rather abrupt departure from CIA custom, these instructions pointed out the probability of an opposition move against Allende and the inevitability that CIA would be blamed as the instigator of any coup.

The Station response to the first message reminded headquarters that CIA continued to have the responsibility of predicting a coup—ringing the gong—and that the Station could hardly be expected to do that unless its agents penetrated all conspiracies.

The second headquarters cable countered this valid argument saying that, this time, keeping CIA's record clean was more important than predicting a coup. In short, the CIA Station Chief was ordered to do the best he could on forecasting a coup from the margin of plotting and to avoid contacts or actions which might be construed as supporting or encouraging those who planned to overthrow Allende.[157]

The United States and the Chilean Opposition: What Does the Evidence Support? The one incontrovertible fact concerning the period after Allende's inauguration that the Church committee uncovered in its investigation was that the CIA had played a crucial role in sustaining the opposition in Chile. But beyond this it offered no standard by which to measure the precise U.S. role in the larger context of developments. To weigh the importance of covert involvement properly, one would have to balance that single fact against several others. For one thing, control of the government armed Popular Unity with significant economic (and therefore political) resources of its own. For another, Allende unquestionably received subsidies of an unknown magnitude from Eastern bloc and Cuban sources. For yet another, there is no inevitable and direct relationship between heavy financial support and political success—as the Watergate affair and the subsequent presidential campaign of John Connally in the United States both illustrate. In Chile it is very possible, as Henry Lansberger has suggested, that foreign influence on one side "simply cancelled out" efforts on the other, "leaving factors internal to Chile as the more basic explanation of what occurred."[158]

Certainly one cannot automatically elide support for the opposition into support for a military coup—as the Church committee comes perilously close to doing any number of times—and then from there jump directly to the event itself. Quite apart from the fact that both the opposition and the armed forces shifted their stance toward the regime over time, CIA practice consistently differentiated between the purposes of the United States and the evolving goals of Chilean actors. Thus the agency withheld money from potential strikers, was repeatedly reminded by headquarters that support for a coup was not authorized, and—in the final, critical weeks of the regime—directly distanced itself from officers known to favor a coup and to be actively discussing that option. Finally, there is no inconsistency whatever between a U.S. policy aimed at "maintaining the democratic opposition for the 1976 election" (Kissinger) and covertly subsidizing hard-pressed political parties, newspapers, and radio stations. Indeed, one can hardly imagine what *other* course of action—given that objective—the U.S. government could have been expected to take. Conversely, if a military coup (as opposed to contingency planning and intelligence gathering) was what Washington wished, why did the 40 Committee so persistently withhold what it could so easily have given—the necessary authorization?

The U.S. Role in Chile: Some Concluding Observations

What is truly remarkable about the investigation of the Church committee of U.S. involvement in Chile is how little its actual findings have altered the perceptions originally created by Representative Harrington's letter and Seymour Hersh's articles in the *New York Times*. For although the United States looked with extreme disfavor on the advent of a socialist government in Chile, it was unable to prevent Allende's election or confirmation by Congress. Nor was it able to facilitate a coup, of either the military or "constitutionalist" variety. Plans to "unleash economic chaos" (ITT) or "make the economy scream" (Nixon)—both conceived during the period between Allende's election and inauguration—remained on the drawing board because of the unwillingness of the banks and major multinationals (with the sole exception of ITT) to endanger their holdings or their future relations with the new government.

Now, eventually the economy did "scream," but not as a result of U.S. government measures. There was no "invisible blockade," either of credit or of spare parts; there *was* a significant reduction (but not a total cutoff) of U.S. public aid to Chile, intensifying a trend already at work during the final year of the Frei regime. There was also a credit squeeze that eventually assumed major proportions, largely as a consequence of the Allende government's own spending policies, which forced it to declare a moratorium on its foreign debt in November 1971. Although failure to reach an agreement with Washington within the context of the Paris club agreements grievously damaged Popular Unity's credit standing in the United States, it nonetheless afforded it very considerable short-term relief.

The U.S. government in all probability did lobby at the Inter-American Development Bank and may also have made attempts at the World Bank to shut off the flow of loans to Chile, but after 1971 such efforts—given the country's general economic perspective—would have been wholly gratuitous. In any event, the attitude of the multilateral banks was of less than critical significance; Chile was able to turn elsewhere for credit, which it obtained in unprecedented amounts. The new terms were considerably less favorable than those traditionally obtained from U.S. sources, but so, indeed, were Chile's prospects for repayment.

Throughout the Popular Unity period the United States expended nearly $6 million to keep opposition political parties and forces alive. This subvention was most evident in the media, interest groups, and the electoral process. The CIA did not, however, generally fund groups committed to the violent overthrow of the regime, such as Patria y Libertad, and although its relations with the Chilean military after the Schneider debacle apparently experienced several shifts, by mid-1972 they were confined to contingency planning and intelligence gathering (monitoring coup plotting). The authorization to go beyond this was pointedly refused several times, and in the final six months of the regime the Santiago station was specifically enjoined to distance itself from coup-prone elements in the armed forces, lest U.S. policy be misunderstood.

The CIA was not involved in promoting or sustaining the strike of October 1972, and although support for that of July–September 1973 was discussed in Washington, no decision was ever reached. The CIA did not, contrary to Seymour Hersh's report, "provide strike benefits for anti-Allende strikers and other workers in 1972 and 1973." [159]

Without question, these activities did have an impact in Chile, though not precisely in the fashion often suggested by critics. Subventions to elements of the opposition created difficulties for the regime, inasmuch as it found itself unable effectively to bankrupt or expropriate their sources of financial support. Allende was therefore forced to implement his policies—policies for which there was no majority—within the context of a continuing pluralistic political system. That is not, however, the same thing as "destabilizing" a regime. As a matter of fact, there never was a decision to "destabilize" Chile. As William Colby later explained in a letter to the *New York Times* on September 18, 1974, the word was Harrington's in *his* characterization of the CIA chief's secret testimony. [160]

One might argue—as Harrington later did—that given the role the United States had played in Chile, withdrawal of support for any regime was bound to have far-reaching (and negative) consequences. But this amounts to nothing more than declaring the obvious—that the United States could have made life much easier for Allende by rushing forward with credits, grants, and other forms of material assistance. It had done this for Frei, in a vain attempt to provide an attractive alternative to Castroism in Latin America. But this perspective does not explain why the United States, having failed to avert the triumph of Marxism in Chile (at the cost of $2 billion in aid and millions more in Overseas Private Investment Corporation insurance premiums), should have ratified its error by throwing good money after bad. This point of view could only make sense if one believed (as Harrington surely does not) that the advancement of Marxism in Latin America and the third world should be an element of U.S. foreign policy.

Finally, whatever its intentions, the United States was utterly unable to conjure up the fundamental weaknesses of the Allende regime. These were a failure to obtain a decisive mandate at the ballot box, a governing coalition internally inconsistent and frequently at war with its constituent elements, an economic policy bound to polarize both its supporters and its enemies, and ultimately the need to recur to the military for the stability that only a genuine consensus could provide. It was here—not in the machinations of the CIA, real or (more often) imagined—that the seeds of disaster were planted. It is to these elements—not to external forces—that anyone wishing to understand the fall of Allende must inevitably recur.

Notes

1. Jack Anderson, *Washington Post*, March 22, 1972.

2. The investigation and the documents were subsequently published as U.S. Congress, Senate, Committee on Foreign Relations, Subcommittee on Multinational Corporations, *The International Telephone and Telegraph Company and Chile, 1970–71,* 93d Congress, 1st session, 1973; a separate report of findings appeared under the same source and title as a committee print on June 21, 1973. Hereafter the hearings and documents are cited as *ITT, 1970–71;* the committee print is cited as *ITT-CP*.

3. Seymour Hersh, *New York Times*, September 20, 1974.

4. Seymour Hersh, *New York Times*, September 24, 1974.

5. The precise designation of the documents is as follows: U.S. Congress, Senate, Select Committee to Study Governmental Operations with Respect to Intelligence Activities, *Covert Action* (Hearings), 94th Congress, 1st session, 1975 (hereafter *Covert Action*); idem, *Alleged Assassination Plots Involv-*

ing Foreign Leaders, 94th Congress, 1st session, 1975 (hereafter *Alleged Assassination Plots*); and idem, *Supplementary Detailed Staff Reports on Foreign and Military Intelligence*, 94th Congress, 2d session, 1976 (hereafter *Supplementary Reports*). The second document deals with alleged assassination plots in many countries; here, obviously, I shall only be concerned with its findings as they apply to Chile.

6. U.S. Congress, House of Representatives, Committee on Foreign Affairs, *The United States and Chile during the Allende Years*, 94th Congress, 1st session, 1975 (hereafter *The United States and Chile*).

7. President Carter at his press conference the next day characterized the Church committee as not having found "any evidence that the U.S. was involved in the overthrow of the Allende government in Chile." The United States had apparently given financial aid to "political elements that may have contributed to the change of government" in Chile, the president admitted, but he said that there had not been "any proof of illegalities here," which was surely beside the point. Ironically, President Carter's statement on that occasion was considerably at variance with his version of Chilean events as he expounded them in his 1976 debate with President Ford. At that time he accused the Republican administration of having "overthrown an elected government and helped to establish a dictatorship" in Chile. All quotations are from *Facts on File, 1977* (New York, 1978), p. 219.

8. *New York Times*, June 3, 4, 1980.

9. Barbara Tuchman, "Kissinger: Self-Portrait," in *Practicing History* (New York: Knopf, 1981), p. 223.

10. *Covert Action*, p. 45.

11. Edward M. Korry, "U.S. Policies in Chile under the Allende Government" (interview with William F. Buckley, Jr., on September 29, 1974), in F. Orrego Vicuna, ed., *Chile: The Balanced View* (Santiago: University of Chile Institute of International Studies, 1975), p. 292.

12. One of the problems with the Church committee report (*Covert Action in Chile, 1963–73* [Washington, 1975]) (hereafter *Covert Action in Chile*) is that it elides CIA activities of the 1960s with those of the Allende period, even though they unfolded under very different conditions. As will be shown further on, it is far easier to defend the necessity of covert action during the Allende period than in the years preceding it.

13. William E. Colby and Peter Forbath, *Honorable Men: My Life in the CIA* (New York: Simon & Schuster, 1978), p. 191. For a fascinating personal account of how one agency official operated in Chile during the early 1950s, see David Atlee Phillips, *The Night Watch: Twenty-five Years of Peculiar Service* (New York: Athens, 1977), pp. 14–28.

14. *Alleged Assassination Plots*, p. 229n; *Covert Action in Chile*, p. 9.

15. Colby and Forbath, *Honorable Men*, p. 302.

16. *Covert Action*, p. 6.

17. *Covert Action in Chile*, p. 16.

18. Ibid., pp. 16–17.

19. Ibid., p. 9.

112

20. Korry, "U.S. Policies in Chile," pp. 289–90.

21. U.S. Congress, Senate, Committee on Foreign Relations, *Nomination of Hon. Cyrus R. Vance to be Secretary of State* (Hearings), 95th Congress, 1st session, 1977 (hereafter *Vance Nomination*), p. 51; *ITT, 1970–71*, vol. 1, pp. 281, 311. In the latter hearings Ambassador Korry remarked that representatives of all three candidates in the 1970 elections approached representatives of major U.S. financial interests in Chile as well.

22. Ambassador Korry estimates $425,000 (*Vance Nomination,* p. 52); *Alleged Assassination Plots,* pp. 20–21, 229, refers to $390,000 with an additional contingency fund of $500,000 set aside to influence the vote of Congress if Allende received a plurality; and *Covert Action in Chile,* p. 20, gives the high figure of "between $800,000 and $1,000,000."

23. *Covert Action* (testimony of Inderfurth), p. 13.

24. *Vance Nomination,* p. 52; *Covert Action in Chile,* pp. 12–13.

25. *Covert Action in Chile,* pp. 12–13; see also *The United States and Chile* (testimony of Sigmund), p. 245.

26. Henry Kissinger, *White House Years* (Boston: Little, Brown, 1979), p. 659.

27. *Covert Action in Chile,* p. 20.

28. Colby and Forbath, *Honorable Men,* pp. 302–3.

29. *Covert Action in Chile,* pp. 17, 19–20.

30. Cord Meyer, *Facing Reality* (New York: Harper & Row, 1980), p. 182.

31. Kissinger, *White House Years,* p. 663.

32. Ibid., p. 665.

33. Ibid., p. 667.

34. Ibid., p. 669.

35. Ibid., pp. 670–71.

36. *ITT, 1970–71,* vol. 1 (testimony of Broe), pp. 244–46.

37. *Covert Action in Chile,* pp. 12–13.

38. *ITT, 1970–71,* vol. 2, pp. 608–15.

39. Ibid., vol. 1 (testimony of McCone), pp. 102–3.

40. Ibid. (testimony of Neal), pp. 59–87; (testimony of Meyer), pp. 398–410; and vol. 2, pp. 599–600.

41. Ibid., pp. 622–23.

42. Ibid., vol. 1 (testimony of Broe), pp. 250–53.

43. *ITT-CP,* p. 11.

44. *ITT, 1970–71,* vol. 2, p. 627 (emphasis added).

45. Ibid., pp. 644–45.

46. *ITT-CP,* p. 11. See also the testimony of various bank executives in *ITT, 1970–71,* vol. 1 (Clark, Lillicotch, Greene, and Ogden), pp. 342–73; (Bolin, Raddatz), pp. 383–98.

47. As William H. Bolin, senior vice-president of the Bank of America, explained to the Church committee, any policy to undermine the Chilean economy "would have been directly contrary to our own interests at that point in time, because we had every reason to expect that we would be approached by the Chilean Government with a proposal to sell out our

branches and that we would be able to negotiate this satisfactorily if the environment of our negotiations were right, and that, in fact, did occur." *ITT, 1970–71,* vol. 1, p. 388.

48. Ibid. (testimony of Greene), p. 359.

49. Ibid. (testimony of Clark), p. 344.

50. To be sure, there were signs of massive bank withdrawals during the period after the September 4 election, but these were due to legitimate fears that Allende would rigorously fulfill his campaign promise to lower interest rates drastically. Broe emphasized in his testimony that this was a preexisting reality upon which the CIA had hoped to build the larger plan he presented to Gerrity. Ibid., pp. 250–51.

51. Ibid., vol. 2, p. 528.

52. Ibid., vol. 1 (testimony of Merriam), pp. 45–47.

53. Ibid. (testimony of Mecham), pp. 265–76.

54. Ibid., (testimony of Foster), pp. 373–77.

55. For example, Anaconda Vice-President Ralph Mecham stated in his testimony that he found it incomprehensible why the Nixon administration persisted at this time in continuing pipeline aid to Chile. Ibid., p. 267.

56. Ibid., p. 320.

57. Ibid. (testimony of Raddatz), p. 393.

58. *Covert Action in Chile,* p. 23; *Alleged Assassination Plots,* p. 225.

59. Kissinger himself describes the September 15 meeting at the White House in somewhat different terms. In his recollection, Nixon "told Helms that he wanted a major effort to see what could be done to prevent Allende's accession to power. . . . Helms should bypass Korry and report directly to the White House, which would make the final decisions. The operational object at the time was still the 'Rube Goldberg' scheme [that is, the Alessandri gambit]. Nixon did not in fact put forward a concrete scheme, only a passionate desire, unfocused and born of frustration, to do 'something.'" In Kissinger's view either Track I or Track II would have involved military participation of some sort; therefore, the Church committee labels are not very meaningful. (Kissinger, *White House Years,* p. 673.) But at best this would not deny the coup-oriented objective of Track II, merely extend it to Track I, which is, by the way, also at times the position of the Church committee. It found, for example, that "the essential difference between Tracks I and II . . . was not that Track II was coup-oriented and Track I was not. Both had this objective in mind. The difference between the two tracks was, simply, that the CIA's direct contacts with the Chilean military and its active promotion and support of a coup *without* President Frei's involvement were to be known only to a small group of individuals in the White House and the CIA." *Alleged Assassination Plots,* p. 232.

Ambassador Korry disagrees. "Track I," he told the Church committee, "followed Mr. Frei, then the President of Chile and its constitutional leader. It adopted certain minimal and cosmetic suggestions put forward by one purportedly in President Frei's confidence. . . . Track II, on the other hand, did not deal with Frei, did not seek his concurrence, did not follow his lead,

114

did not pretend to be within any constitutional framework of Chile." *Covert Action*, pp. 30–31 (emphasis added). Of course, Korry only learned of the existence of Track II some years later.

60. *Alleged Assassination Plots*, p. 230.

61. Kissinger, *White House Years*, pp. 674–75.

62. The full statement, originally passed to Frei through his defense minister, read: "Frei should know that not a nut or bolt will be allowed to reach Chile under Allende. Once Allende comes to power we shall do all within our power to condemn Chile and Chileans to utmost deprivation and poverty, a policy designed for a long time to come to accelerate the hard features of a Communist society in Chile. Hence, for Frei to believe that there will be much of an alternative to utter misery, such as seeing Chile through, would be strictly illusory." Quoted in *Alleged Assassination Plots*, p. 231n. Korry later explained to the Church committee that the statement was a "deliberate overstatement" to goad Frei into activity along Track I (the "Alessandri gambit") and relieve Korry of pressures emanating from Washington "to go to the military" (the "constitutional" coup). *Supplementary Reports*, pp. 127–28.

63. *Alleged Assassination Plots*, pp. 232–33.

64. *Covert Action in Chile*, pp. 23–24.

65. Meyer, *Facing Reality*, pp. 185–86; see also *Covert Action in Chile*, pp. 33–37.

66. In its report, the Church committee went to considerable lengths to establish that these two groups were not totally discrete entities. (See especially *Alleged Assassination Plots*, p. 239, n. 2); nonetheless, they were treated as such by the CIA and, as will be shown, operated as if they were.

67. Kissinger, *White House Years*, p. 676.

68. *Alleged Assassination Plots*, p. 243.

69. Ibid., pp. 243–45.

70. Ibid., p. 226.

71. Ibid., n.

72. *Covert Action in Chile*, p. 24.

73. *Alleged Assassination Plots*, p. 246. There may have been more to this episode than immediately meets the eye. For example, Ambassador Korry explained in a letter to Senator Church on September 23, 1975, that "Track II slid into a trap to which I had oft alluded in my cables since 1969—that the extreme Left had infiltrated the military plotters to encourage sedition and that it also acted, or would act, as agents-provocateurs. In the incident which ended with the murder of General Schneider . . . the extreme Left was very much involved. Indeed, the Allende government was remarkably lenient in its punishment of Schneider's killers [Viaux, as 'intellectual author' of the crime, was sentenced to five years' exile] and those incriminated because, among other considerations, the military investigators who tracked and named the murderers and their accomplices discovered the links to extreme Left activists who were intimates of, and supporters of, Allende." Text in *Covert Action*, p. 122.

74. *ITT, 1970–71*, vol. 1 (testimony of Guilfoyle), p. 208.

75. *ITT-CP*, pp. 13–16; U.S. Congress, House of Representatives, Committee on Foreign Affairs, Subcommittee on Inter-American Affairs, *Recent Developments in Chile*, 92d Congress, 1st session, 1971 (hereafter *Recent Developments*) (testimony of Mays), p. 6.

76. Embassy of Chile (Washington), press release, text in *ITT, 1970–71*, vol. 1, pp. 228–29.

77. Korry, "U.S. Policies in Chile," p. 292. Whether the U.S. taxpayer should in effect have borne the burden of such risks is a debatable matter, although at the time such insurance was introduced it was believed that it would defuse potentially explosive investment disputes. Instead of isolating the sources of conflict, however, OPIC insurance in effect spread them into the political community, where elected representatives were bound to get involved. This curious bifurcation of intentions and results is fully explored in Paul Sigmund, *Multinationals in Latin America* (Madison: University of Wisconsin Press, 1980), esp. pp. 302–37.

78. See excerpted texts, "The Nixon-Frost Interviews," *Historic Documents of 1977* (Washington, D.C.: 1978), pp. 351–52; Congressional Quarterly, "The Foreign Policy of the Popular Unity Government," in Federico Gil et al., *Chile at the Turning Point* (Philadelphia: Institute for the Study of Human Issues, 1979), p. 101.

79. Korry, "U.S. Policies in Chile," pp. 294–95.

80. Richard Nixon, "Third Annual Report to the Congress of the United States on Foreign Policy, February 9, 1972," in *Public Papers of the Presidents of the United States: Richard Nixon, 1972* (Washington, 1974), pp. 263–64. Much has been made since Allende's fall of the hypocrisy of this statement; nonetheless, in diplomacy as in everything else, deception is a game any number can play. President Allende, too, made florid statements affirming his desire for cordial relations with the United States but, when offered the opportunity to reach an accommodation in early 1971—in the concrete matter of compensation for U.S. mining properties—found himself unable to proceed. This was due to pressures from within the left wing of his own coalition, which, as Almeyda has since complained, was quick to see an "unjustifiable surrender in every negotiation and compromise." ("Foreign Policy of the Popular Unity Government," p. 85.) Doubtless Allende was sincere in his desire to minimize conflict with the United States, *as long as it cost him nothing.* "I don't know of a single instance," Ambassador Korry remarked to a U.S. congressional committee in mid-1971, "where the President of Chile has assured me or where his ambassador assured the Department [of State] of something that was going to happen that has happened yet, not a single instance where it involves our interests. . . . It just hasn't worked out ever that their assurances have been fulfilled. . . . I think when the President of Chile gives me these assurances, he is being sincere about them, but because of these internal contradictions within his own government . . . he can't carry them out." (*The United States and Chile*, p. 16.) For its part, the Nixon administration proceeded on the basis of a worst-case scenario; but had its olive branch not been so summarily rejected, events might have acquired a momentum of

116

their own. In any event, the darkest forebodings of Washington proved justified by subsequent Chilean actions. Ambassador Korry is preparing a memoir on this subject; pending its publication, readers are referred to his remarks in "U.S. Policies in Chile," pp. 291–94; *Covert Action*, pp. 32–33; and "Ambassador Korry on a 1971 Proposal to Allende," *Washington Post*, September 29, 1974.

81. "Sobre la independencia política y económica de los pueblos" [On the political and economic independence of peoples], official text released by Chilean mission to the United Nations, mimeographed.

82. *Alleged Assassination Plots*, p. 227.

83. *Covert Action in Chile*, p. 33.

84. Jonathan E. Sanford, "The Multilateral Development Banks and the Suspension of Lending to Allende's Chile," in Orrego Vicuna, *Chile: The Balanced View*, pp. 127–30. Although this is an official Chilean government publication, Sanford's work is merely reprinted. It was originally commissioned by the Congressional Research Service in Washington, D.C.

85. Belgium, Canada, France, Great Britain, Italy, Japan, the Netherlands, Spain, Switzerland, West Germany, and, of course, the United States.

86. Virginia M. Hagen, "United States Relations with Chile under the Government of Salvador Allende: Background and Current Developments," in *The United States and Chile*, p. 401; Nathaniel Davis, "U.S. Covert Actions in Chile, 1971–73," *Foreign Service Journal* (November 1978), p. 38; $243 million is the figure estimated by the International Monetary Fund.

87. "Background Paper: Chile and the Inter-American Development Bank during the Administration of President Salvador Allende," in *The United States and Chile*, pp. 440–41.

88. Sanford, "Multilateral Development Banks," pp. 137–40.

89. International Bank for Reconstruction and Development (IBRD), "Chile and the World Bank," in *The United States and Chile*, pp. 441–48.

90. The space was actually of three weeks' duration. The Special Copper Tribunal refused to hear the appeals of the American companies on October 14, 1971. The next day a special World Bank mission returned to Washington from Chile and reported on the inadvisability of new loans to that country. Chile suspended service on its public foreign debt on November 9.

91. Sanford, "Multilateral Development Banks," p. 137.

92. IBRD,"Chile and the World Bank," p. 447. The annual average under Frei was $15.6 million, under Allende $15.4 million.

93. "The Nixon-Frost Interviews," p. 351.

94. It is not clear that it would have made much difference if they had. At a confidential meeting with representatives of major American investors in Chile on October 21, 1971, Secretary of State William Rogers, Jr., turned aside pressures "to curtail IADB [IDB] loans" with the remark that the United States "does not have veto power over loans." *ITT, 1970–71*, vol. 2, p. 975.

95. Paul Sigmund, *The Overthrow of Allende* (Pittsburgh: University of Pittsburgh Press, 1977), p. 338.

96. See, for example, the figures offered by William S. Ogden, executive

vice-president of Chase Manhattan, in *ITT, 1970–71*, vol. 1, pp. 366–67.

97. Ibid., vol. 1 (testimony of Bolin), pp. 386–92.

98. Alexis Guardia, "Structural Transformations in Chile's Economy and Its System of External Economic Relations," in S. Sideri, ed., *Chile, 1970–73: Economic Development and Its International Setting* (The Hague: Martinus Nijhoff, 1979), p. 76.

99. *ITT, 1970–71*, vol. 1 (testimony of Greene), p. 360; (testimony of Ogden), pp. 366–73; (testimony of Bolin), pp. 386–87; and vol. 2, p. 536.

100. *Covert Action in Chile*, pp. 32–33.

101. This would have run the eventual risk of renewed legal action by the copper companies and would also have necessitated relocating specialized personnel already settled in New York. But since it was never tried, we cannot know to what degree these obstacles would have been negotiated successfully.

102. Carlos Fortín, "Nationalization of Copper in Chile and Its International Repercussions," in Sideri, *Chile, 1970–73*, pp. 207–8; and Fernando Fajnzylber, "The External Sector and the Policies of the Unidad Popular Government," in ibid., pp. 144–45.

103. "Copper Is the Wage of Chile," *American Universities Field Staff Reports* (West Coast South America Series), vol. 19, no. 3 (1972), p. 10.

104. *ITT, 1970–71*, vol. 2, p. 1074.

105. Ibid., p. 1075.

106. For a persuasive but fundamentally misleading account of this issue from a pro-Allende point of view, see Edward Boorstein, *Allende's Chile* (New York: International Publishers, 1977), pp. 89–107. It is worth noting that the issue of spare parts was not seen as a particularly conflictive element in U.S.-Chilean relations *at the time*; instead, many Chilean officials effusively welcomed the opportunity to diversify their country's foreign sources of supply. It was only after the fall of the regime that this issue surfaced as an element in the debate, suggesting its polemical rather than concrete value.

107. These figures are from Kenneth Ruddle and Kathleen Barrows, eds., *Statistical Abstract of Latin America, 1972* (Los Angeles: UCLA Latin American Center, 1974), table 276; and James Wilkie and Paul Turovsky, eds., *Statistical Abstract of Latin America, 1976* (Los Angeles: UCLA Latin American Center, 1976), table 3000.

108. U.S. Arms Control and Disarmament Agency, *World Military Expenditures and Arms Transfers, 1966–75* (Washington, D.C., 1976), table II.

109. Davis, "U.S. Covert Actions in Chile," p. 39.

110. *ITT, 1970–71*, vol. 1 (testimony of Hennessy), p. 340.

111. Paul Sigmund, "The 'Invisible Blockade' and the Overthrow of Allende," *Foreign Affairs*, vol. 52, no. 2 (1974), p. 334.

112. Sigmund, *The Overthrow of Allende*, p. 153. For alternative explanations of the transaction offered by Export-Import Bank officials, see *Recent Developments* (testimony of Sauer), pp. 5–6; and U.S. Congress, House of Representatives, Committee on Foreign Affairs, Subcommittee on Inter-American Affairs, *New Directions for the 1970s: Part 2, Developmental Assistance*

Options in Latin America, 92d Congress, 1st session, 1971 (testimony of Corette), p. 225.

113. After discussions with the Soviets, the Chileans returned to Boeing in early 1972 and purchased the three planes with funds that, "according to speculation," could have come out of a $50 million credit from Moscow. Hagen, "United States Relations with Chile," p. 400.

114. Philip O'Brien, "Was the United States Responsible for the Chilean Coup?" in Philip O'Brien, ed., *Allende's Chile* (New York: Praeger, 1976), p. 233.

115. *Covert Action in Chile*, p. 32.

116. *The United States and Chile* (testimony of Crimmins), p. 69.

117. "Foreign Policy of the Popular Unity Government," p. 87.

118. Ibid., pp. 89–90.

119. Ibid., p. 93.

120. Guardia, "Structural Transformations in Chile's Economy," p. 85.

121. Ibid., p. 86.

122. International Monetary Fund, *International Financial Statistics, 1973 Supplement* (Washington, D.C.: IMF, n.d.), p. 71.

123. Guardia, "Structural Transformations in Chile's Economy," pp. 82–83.

124. See, for example, the critique by Ronald I. McKinnon, *Money in International Exchange* (New York: Oxford University Press, 1979), pp. 50–67.

125. *The United States and Chile* (testimony of Crimmins), p. 69. For a similar observation with respect to Western Europe, see Guardia, "Structural Transformations in Chile's Economy," p. 86.

126. O'Brien, "Was the United States Responsible?" p. 233. An explanation of the more advantageous role formerly played by American banks is presented in *ITT, 1970–71* (testimony of Greene), p. 363.

127. There was, he adds, a slight decline in sales to Western Europe and the United States, but this was compensated for by increased shipments to Japan, Latin America, and the socialist countries, particularly China. Fortín, "Nationalization of Copper in Chile," pp. 205, 206–7.

128. Guardia, "Structural Transformations in Chile's Economy," p. 86.

129. Clive Bell and David Lehmann, "The International Context of *La Vía Chilena*," in J. Ann Zammit, ed., *The Chilean Road to Socialism* (Brighton, Sussex: Institute for Development Studies, 1973), p. 359n.

130. Markos J. Mamalakis, *The Growth and Structure of the Chilean Economy* (New Haven, Conn.: Yale University Press, 1976), pp. 260–61.

131. These fell from $219 million in August 1970 to $32 million in August 1972.

132. *The United States and Chile* (testimony of Crimmins), p. 69; (testimony of Lansberger), pp. 227–28; Henry A. Lansberger, "An Introduction to the Complexities of Assessing the U.S. Credit Squeeze," in *The United States and Chile*, pp. 527–28; and Guardia, "Structural Transformations in Chile's Economy," pp. 83, 86.

133. *Covert Action in Chile*, p. 27.

134. *The United States and Chile* (testimony of Sigmund), p. 247.

135. *Covert Action* (testimony of Treverton), p. 16. Some additional funds were spent for propaganda activities of a more general sort. According to the Church committee, the CIA also (1) subsidized several magazines of national circulation and a large number of books and special studies; (2) developed material for placement in opposition press and electronic media; and (3) funded an opposition research organization that channeled a steady flow of economic and technical material to opposition parties and private sector groups. Many bills introduced by opposition parliamentarians were drafted by this organization. *Covert Action in Chile*, p. 30.

136. By the end of the regime *El Mercurio*, normally comparable in size to the *Washington Post*, was reduced to an edition of six to eight pages, virtually devoid of advertising.

137. Davis, "U.S. Covert Actions," p. 11; Everett G. Martin, "Did the Chilean Press Need CIA Help?" *Wall Street Journal*, September 18, 1974.

138. *Covert Action* (testimony of Treverton), p. 17.

139. Ibid. (testimony of Korry), p. 4. See also Ambassador Korry's letter to Senator Church dated October 23, 1975, reprinted in ibid., p. 117; and his remarks to William Buckley, Jr., in Korry, "U.S. Policies in Chile," pp. 296–97.

140. Nathaniel Davis, "U.S. Covert Actions in Chile, 1971–73, Part II," *Foreign Service Journal* (December 1978), p. 11; *Covert Action in Chile*, pp. 10, 28–29.

141. *Covert Action in Chile*, pp. 31, 49.

142. Davis, "U.S. Covert Actions," p. 14.

143. Korry, letter to Senator Church.

144. Davis, "U.S. Covert Actions, Part II," p. 11.

145. *Covert Action in Chile*, pp. 16, 22, 30–31.

146. Ibid., p. 31.

147. Davis, "U.S. Covert Actions, Part II," p. 14.

148. *Covert Action in Chile*, p. 10.

149. Ibid., pp. 30–31.

150. Phillips, *The Night Watch*, p. 237.

151. *Covert Action in Chile*, p. 2.

152. *Alleged Assassination Plots*, p. 254. Asterisks indicate material excised by the editors of the report.

153. *Covert Action in Chile*, p. 37 (emphasis added).

154. Ibid., pp. 38–39.

155. Ibid. (emphasis added).

156. Ibid., p. 135.

157. Phillips, *The Night Watch*, p. 238.

158. *The United States and Chile* (testimony of Lansberger), p. 226.

159. Hersh's other sensational allegation—that Ambassador Davis at some point was instructed "to aid the opposition by any means possible" and "to get a little rougher"—was flatly denied by Davis at the time his articles were published and, as the ambassador later had the satisfaction of observing,

found no substantiation in the Senate investigation. "U.S. Covert Actions in Chile," p. 38.

160. To insure that no mere difference in semantics is involved," Colby added, "this term especially is not a fair description of our national policy [in Chile] from 1971 on of encouraging the continued existence of democratic forces looking to future elections." Newsman Daniel Schorr, who was later also permitted to read top secret materials on covert CIA operations in Chile, has corroborated Colby's statement. Daniel Schorr, *Clearing the Air* (Nashville, Tenn.: Aurora Publications, 1977), pp. 130–33.

Index

124

A NOTE ON THE BOOK

This book was edited by Gertrude Kaplan
and by Sayre Ellen Dykes of the
Publications Staff of the American Enterprise Institute.
The staff also designed the cover and format, with Pat Taylor.
The text was set in Palatino, a typeface designed by Hermann Zapf.
Hendricks-Miller Typographic Company, of Washington, D.C.,
set the type, and Thomson-Shore, Inc., of Dexter, Michigan,
printed and bound the book, using Glatfelter paper.